SCALING A CITY

1958–2013: The First 55 Years of the
Cleveland Baptist Church

This book is lovingly dedicated to the group of people who were here from the earliest days of Cleveland Baptist Church. I am speaking specifically of those who were in the house on Memphis Avenue, those who became a part of the church in the theater building, and those who were there 50 years ago when the church celebrated its fifth anniversary.

Every church has a beginning, and it takes special people to come in when a church is young and share the vision of the man of God that a church is needed. These people sacrificed to get things off the ground. These people scrimped and saved, labored and prayed. Of those who were there in those early days, just a handful remain. A good number of that early group has been called home to heaven and are rejoicing around the throne of God. To those that remain, we are grateful, and we are honored to tell the story that you have lived.

Those of us who are a part of Cleveland Baptist Church today owe so much to those that have been a part from the beginning! Thank you!

Dr. Kevin Folger
Senior Pastor

ACKKNOWLEDGEMENTS

The following individuals contributed much-needed support to this project. Their help is most appreciated and the final product would not have been possible without them:

Pastor Folger, Faith Thompson, Joyce, Bruce and Becky Witzke, Larry Clayton, Dan Wolvin, Bruce Musselman, Nancy Folger, Pete Folger, Kristina Premo, Luke and Pam Brown, Christine Aichele, Leah Kardamis, Jack Beaver, David Gibbs Jr., Ron Van Kirk, Chris Ruscitto, Roger and Joyce Hoffman, Brian Starre, Jim Jones, Cheryl Williamson, Garry Douglas Jr., Linda Montgomery, Steve Triplett, Rick Pflaum, Craig Parker, Alyssa Jonke

Table of Contents

Twenty years ago, when Cleveland Baptist Church was celebrating its 35th anniversary, Mrs. Linda Montgomery took the time to write the history of the church. While it is not typical to make much of a 35th anniversary, we were well aware that Dr. Roy Thompson was in his final years as senior pastor. It was important to us then to make sure honor was given to the man God had used to establish this church that has touched so many lives. A lot has happened since that last book, and we thought it only fitting to update the history on the occasion of the 55th anniversary.

I want to thank Brother Drew Jonke for undertaking this important task of chronicling the history of Cleveland Baptist Church. God has gifted him with the ability to write and tell the story. We want you to know that in a book of this size and this nature it is impossible to tell every story and mention every person that played a part in these first 55 years. If a person or event is not mentioned, it does not mean that event or person was not important. It simply means that we could include only so many stories in this limited amount of space. Please be understanding of that fact as you read.

More than anything else, it is important to us that God is honored by this history. It is true that God uses men to accomplish His plan; yet, it is God, first and foremost, Who should receive the honor.

I trust that you will enjoy this book as you read about God's miracle work in Cleveland, Ohio.

Dr. Kevin Folger
Senior Pastor

A 33-page booklet called *Commitment for Life* was written by Linda Montgomery in 1993. After conducting a number of interviews, I have taken this content and edited, expanded, and added to it. Some of the information presented has not been formally documented and is therefore subject to the memory of those involved. While a significant effort has been made to ensure correctness, it is possible that one reader may remember something differently than another. I believe the material to be accurate in its entirety, but evidence was not available to capture every detail "beyond a shadow of a doubt." It is my request that each reader keep this in mind while reading.

Drew Jonke

Scaling a City

A wise man scaleth the city of the mighty, and casteth down the strength of the confidence thereof.—Proverbs 21:22

Strength trumps weakness, but wisdom trumps strength. While the Bible believer recognizes that Jesus Christ's strength is made perfect in weakness (2 Corinthians 12:9), the Holy Spirit through Solomon points out in Proverbs 21:22 that wisdom is more valuable than physical strength. He alluded to an ancient battle in which one army storms the gates of a city. The one described as wise is victorious over those described as mighty. Even if those defending the city are vastly superior in brute force, they will be no match against a cunning, sly opponent. This is why strength is not the principal thing, but wisdom is (Proverbs 4:7). The wise leader creates an advantage by outthinking his foe. In the War for Independence, the colonists were outnumbered, but they consistently outsmarted the British. Though they lost in the end, the Confederates were outnumbered in countless battles in the American Civil War, but their generals outfoxed the Federals. The top coaches in sports are able to tactically outmaneuver their opponents. Physical strength eventually fades while wisdom remains.

The argument cannot be made that Solomon was talking about church planting or soulwinning, but this truth of God's Word does apply when God sends a man to a city to reach its people with the gospel. If a man has obeyed God's call, he is wise; for the fear of the Lord is the beginning of wisdom (Proverbs 9:10). In the New Testament sense, this wise man is not there to engage in a physical struggle with the mighty men. Contrary to the false religions of the world, the New Testament doesn't say, "If they disagree with you, beat them up or imprison them." Rather, the wise man is there to cast down the strength in which the mighty men have placed their confidence.

With regard to their eternal soul and where they're going when they die, all men have their confidence in something. If everyone in the city already believed the gospel, God wouldn't have to send His wise man to it. The city needs to be scaled because its men are trusting in their might. They are trusting in that which is physical. Their confidence is in their works, in a religious rite, or in evolution. These are all physical. The wise man is sent to cast down the strength of these false confidences. To be saved, men must have the strength of their own confidence cast down. They must admit, "I can't do it."

When a man brings the gospel of Jesus Christ to a city, there may be physical walls to scale, but there will certainly be spiritual walls to scale. False religions and erroneous belief systems build walls. No person enjoys being told his confidence is misplaced. Most people build defensive walls to protect their comfort zones. It is seldom easy, but fortunately, walls *can* be scaled. Walls are obstacles, but a wise man understands that reaching the people is worth the effort required to overcome the obstacles. A wise man sees beyond the intimidation of the obstacles and recognizes that wisdom beats strength because the spiritual beats the physical. He is outnumbered; "man" in the verse is singular, but it is a place "of the mighty," which refers to plural men. God specializes in delivering when His man depends on Him alone to overcome the obstacles.

The following pages tell of a man scaling a city. That man is Roy Thompson, and the city is Cleveland, Ohio. There is, of course, more to the story. It is the story of a church with a burden for the mighty men of its city who need to take their confidence out of something else to place it in Jesus Christ. The church began with one man, but once some mighty men had the strength of their confidence cast down, they joined the wise man. This book is an attempt to capture the process of a city being scaled. As you read, it will be profitable to consider the strategic, godly wisdom employed by the wise as men forsake their own strength.

CHAPTER ONE

A Troubled Home

He that troubleth his own house shall inherit the
wind…—Proverbs 11:29

The year was 1933. The Depression was just beginning to bottom out and America was struggling to get back on its economic feet. The stock market crash of 1929 had virtually paralyzed the entire nation. Employment was at an all-time low, and many men were working various types of menial labor just to put food on the table. In Europe, the winds of war were gathering speed, and in a few short years, those gusts would launch America into World War II. It was under these circumstances that the family of Henry and Mabel Thompson, like many others in Grand Rapids, Michigan, was struggling just to survive.

Henry Gillson Thompson entered the working world in 1922, laboring as a branch connector for the railroad. At the age of 19, while attempting to connect two cars together, a connector slipped and a railway car crushed his leg. He was placed on a flatbed railroad car and rushed to a hospital, but it wasn't soon enough. The damage done to his leg by the accident required amputation. Unable to return to his job at the railroad after the accident, he trained to become a telegraph operator and made his livelihood working for Postal Telegraph until it went out of business.

Mabel Lucille Peterson was a good woman when she met and married Henry Thompson. Her hope and dream was that she and her husband would serve the Lord and raise their children according to the Word of God. During the course of their marriage, Mrs. Thompson gave birth to two sons and one daughter. In 1927, Dorothy was born and in 1929, Mrs. Thompson gave birth to her first son, Andrew.

The Thompson household was what is known today as a dysfunctional family. Henry Thompson had become an alcoholic and spent his hard-earned money to sustain his drinking habit. His wife and two small children were often left for days at a time without food and other necessities of life. When he did come home, his wife and children were met with physical abuse. Many a night, Mabel took the children and fled for safety at the Mel Trotter Rescue Mission.

It was under these conditions that Mabel Thompson found herself to be pregnant for the third time. She suffered complications during this pregnancy, and the doctor told her that there was no way, humanly speaking, to save both her and the baby. A choice had to be made. The doctor reminded her that she had two other children at home that needed her.

Without the support of a loving husband, her heart was heavy as she weighed her options; however, Mabel Thompson believed in the power of God. In tears, alone in the hospital, she bowed her head and prayed, "Lord, I ask that you would let this baby live. If this child is a boy, I pray that you would make his life count for something and call him to be a preacher of your Word." The Lord granted her request to let the baby live, and on May 25, 1933, Henry Roy Thompson made his entrance into the world. God, gracious as He is, went one step further and allowed Mrs. Thompson to live and to see her son become one of the greatest preachers of his time.

Roy Thompson – age 3

Roy Thompson and His Mother, Mabel

CHAPTER TWO

A Changed Direction

*...the blood of Jesus Christ his Son cleanseth us from
all sin.*—I John 1:7

During the course of young Roy's life, his family moved to Akron, Ohio, and finally to Dayton, Ohio. Roy and his family did whatever was necessary to survive. They slept on streets. They begged. They stole. He often chose not to go to school and spent his time in pool halls instead. In 1947, after attending school through ninth grade and at the age of 14, Roy decided he had enough of living in an abusive home. He dropped out of school and, using his brother's birth certificate as his own, joined the armed forces. He wrote to Andrew that he would return his wallet and money later.

Roy was stationed in Kentucky. Due to his strong voice and mature appearance, he often found himself calling out cadence for his company; unfortunately, he was usually in trouble and found himself in the brig on a regular basis. At one point he spent three months in confinement in a military prison. Years later, according to his wife, "I didn't know him yet, but I understand he had a smart mouth on him at that time."

Roy wrote to his mom that his being in the Army "would make a man out of him," but he missed her. Without permission, he left to see her. Having heard that deserters were shot, she was worried. His father wrote to the chaplain, and Roy was discharged at the age of 16. In his letter, his father admitted that he was aware of what had happened, but he had allowed Roy to continue because there were lessons he hoped Roy would learn. In the military, he became a product of his environment. He acquired his father's propensity for alcohol and was well on his way to becoming an alcoholic. He returned to an immoral, drunken lifestyle on the streets after leaving the Army.

Even though Roy's mother's dream of raising her children in a Christian environment never materialized, she remained faithful to the Lord and prayed for her children daily. Andrew had a job at a newspaper, and Roy joined him there. Dorothy married, and she and her husband, Ed Sanderfer, made their home in Akron, Ohio.

Dorothy and Ed soon began attending the Akron Baptist Temple, which had been there since 1934. Even in the midst of the Depression, it was one of the first churches to have a bus ministry. City buses were rented, and the regular city routes were run. People rode free, and thousands came. Akron Baptist Temple built one of the largest Sunday schools in the world, averaging 7,000 (with high days approaching 10,000). It was founded by Dr. Dallas Billington, who had moved to Akron from Kentucky to work in a rubber factory. Dr. Billington, having no formal education, was a large man with a commanding presence. He was strong but meek. He would weep as he explained to people what Jesus did to save them from their sins. Both Dorothy and Ed were saved under his ministry.

Roy was living in Dayton, Ohio in 1952 and occasionally went to Akron to see his sister and brother-in-law, thoroughly enjoying his visits with them. A remarkable change had taken place in their lives, and he wondered what had happened. Ed was no longer drinking, they were teaching Sunday school, and their home seemed so peaceful. On one such visit during the week of Easter, Dorothy begged Roy to attend an evening church service with her and Ed. Roy was a little reluctant. He tried to make the excuse that he didn't have proper clothing to wear to church, but Dorothy persuaded him to go. On that Friday night, Roy found himself sitting about a dozen rows from the front in an auditorium packed with more than 3,000 people.

Akron Baptist Temple was hosting a revival meeting that week. Dr. Billington had invited Dr. B.R. Lakin to be the guest speaker. As Roy sat under his preaching, he couldn't understand how this man knew all about him. He had never heard about a day that was coming whereby all unsaved men would be judged. The "Great White Throne Judgment" was what this preacher was calling it. It sounded ominous, but his message didn't end there. Dr. Lakin quoted verse after verse about the fact that God loved mankind enough to send His only Son to die that mankind might be redeemed. Roy's father had told him only that he hated him. He had never heard such a powerful message of love. The Spirit of God softly spoke to the young man's heart as the Word of God showed him his need for the Savior. In April 1952, with Dr. Jim Moore's arm around him, Roy Thompson knelt at an old-fashioned altar, admitted he was a sinner in desperate need of salvation, and asked the Lord Jesus Christ to save him.

When he left the service that evening, he was a changed man. It was then that he understood what had changed his sister's life. From that point on, he never returned to Dayton, not even to pick up his belongings. He didn't want to go back to a place where he knew Satan would tempt him. He stayed in Akron, lived with Dorothy and Ed, got a job, and began his spiritual growth. Immediately God took liquor and immorality out of his life. Soon thereafter, Roy was baptized and began to attend church faithfully.

God was crafting wisdom in a man that He would send to scale a city.

Roy Thompson - 15 Years Old

Roy Thompson in 1952

Dr. Dallas Billington

Dr. B.R. Lakin

CHAPTER THREE

A True Friend

A friend loveth at all times...—Proverbs 17:17

In the fall of 1952, Roy enrolled in the Bible college that was a ministry of Akron Baptist Temple. The enrollment form asked the question, "Do you use alcohol or tobacco?" He had quit drinking, but cigarettes were his crutch. He had tried unsuccessfully to quit in the past. In fact, he had a pack in his pocket at that very moment. He believed that if he said "Yes," he would not be accepted; but if he said, "No," he would be lying. He said to the Lord, "I promise I will throw them away. I want to go to this college." He answered, "No," and never smoked another cigarette again in his life.

At this same time, Roy's father had become quite ill. His life-long drinking habit had taken its toll on his body, and he was not expected to live very long. After not having seen his father for several years, Roy went to visit him to tell him how God had changed his life. He tried to convince his father that he needed to be saved, but in November of 1952, at the age of 49, Henry Gillson Thompson went out into eternity refusing to accept Jesus Christ as his personal Savior.

In one of Roy's college classes was an 18-year-old farm boy named Larry Clayton from Tawawa, Ohio. Larry had heard about Akron Baptist Temple's Bible college on the radio. He heard that it was free for anyone who was called to preach. That was all the information he needed. He had dug ditches until his hands bled all summer to earn the money he needed to get to Akron.

When Larry arrived in Akron via Greyhound the night before his first day at Bible college, he stayed at the YMCA. He woke up in the middle of the night to the smell of smoke, an odor that was less familiar to him than to Akron natives. In a panic, he dressed, sprinted downstairs, and said the building was on fire. A YMCA employee asked where the fire was. Larry couldn't believe she didn't smell it. She said, "That's the smell of money." He looked puzzled. She told him that tire factories were how they made their money around there. He went back to bed. When he arrived at Akron Baptist Temple the next morning, he had one suit, a belt wrapped around his lone suitcase to keep it closed, and no Bible. He bought a Bible from the bookstore and went without food until he was able to pay for it. Roy and Larry immediately became friends. They would remain friends for the next 58 years.

Roy and Larry formed a little team that would go out and represent the college. On the last evening of 1952, they found themselves at Dayton Baptist Temple. When the calendar page was turned to 1953, Roy Thompson had preached his first sermon. It lasted 12 minutes.

Some nights, Roy and Larry would go to Akron Baptist Temple to pray together. There were times they prayed all night. Roy had experienced a bad life, and his heart was tender toward God for changing it. Larry had experienced a good life, and his heart was tender toward God for providing it. Their life-long friendship was a source of encouragement for them both. Years later, one jealous individual tried to drive a wedge between them. He said to Roy, "Do you know what Larry says about you when you're not around?" Roy trusted Larry and quickly discerned the motive of this instigator. He responded, "No, but Larry knows me better than anybody, so whatever he says about me must be true!"

In April of 1953, Roy was drafted into the Army to serve his country during the Korean conflict. He was somewhat fearful of returning to the armed services for fear that he would not have the opportunity to learn more about the Lord. In addition to that fear, Roy remembered that the Army was where he started drinking. He was determined not to return to that lifestyle. Larry had also been drafted, but obtained a deferment based on his pursuit of a career as a preacher. It helped that the county from which he came had enough volunteers that he was not needed. Roy spoke with Dr. Billington about the draft notice he had received. Dr. Billington told him that his own son had served in the military, and that it was a noble, worthwhile endeavor.

Roy volunteered to go to Korea, hoping that the fear of death would instill a sense of urgency that would be conducive to soulwinning "in the fox hole." The rest of his company went to Korea, but Roy was instead sent to Germany. On the 12-day boat ride, Roy read the New Testament 11 times, often forgoing lunch to feast on spiritual meat. When he arrived in Germany, he learned to speak German and earned his GED. He assisted the chaplain on his base and involved himself in ministry. He joined a Youth-for-Christ program and became one of its primary speakers. He led many soldiers to the Lord.

Roy and Larry stayed in touch by writing. Larry remained in Akron Baptist Temple Bible College while Roy was in Germany, but plans were in place for the college to move to Texas. The two discussed where they would continue their training when Roy returned. Roy told Larry to make that decision for them both. Dr. Billington told Larry that Baptist Bible College in Springfield, Missouri, founded by G.B. Vick, might be the best place for them. Larry could've gone to Baptist Bible College right away, but he waited for his friend. In the meantime, he took classes at Cornus Hill Bible College. After taking a trip to Springfield to see BBC for himself, he wrote to Roy, "That's where we're going to go to school." After 18 months, Roy's stint with the Army was completed because the time he had served under his brother's name was applied to his record.

Upon his honorable discharge, Roy returned to Akron, Ohio in 1954 and found a job at Firestone. His appetite for the Word of God was insatiable, and he enrolled in night classes at Cornus Hill Bible College, while Larry took classes during the day. Most of Larry's young life had been confined to the rural farm lands of western Ohio. Roy was the opposite; he had been all over the United States, had been in Germany, and had seen and heard much of what the world had to offer. Despite being an unlikely duo, the spiritual encouragement they provided for one another was instrumental in their lives.

Roy mentioned to Larry that he'd like to start a church in Cleveland. Men had planted successful churches all over Ohio, but when Roy returned from the military, he couldn't believe that they had gone almost everywhere in the state but Cleveland. It was known as a city of sin, and Roy wanted Cleveland to be transformed the way his own life had been transformed. He and Larry drove the 35 miles that separate the two cities to look around. The pastor of Cleveland Baptist Temple offered Roy a job as his assistant, but he turned it down. The two preacher boys finished their term in Akron with their sights set on Baptist Bible College.

God was preparing Roy Thompson's heart to lead him to a city that needed to be scaled.

Larry Clayton

Cornus Hill Bible College

Cleveland, Ohio

CHAPTER FOUR

A Godly Couple

A time to plant...a time to laugh...a time to embrace....—Ecclesiastes 3:3-5

F aith Diane Sherban was also the product of a broken home. Her parents were divorced when she was just six years old. For most of the remainder of her adolescent years, she was raised by her Romanian grandparents, who lived in Akron, Ohio.

Faith was saved at the age of 16 after an evening service at a Romanian Baptist church where English was barely spoken. An American preached in English about the love of God, and when Faith went home that night, she put her trust in Christ alone. Prior to that, she was able to give proper answers concerning salvation, but she had never personally received the free gift of eternal life. Coincidentally, she was saved the same week and year that Roy was saved. Because her church mostly ministered to people who spoke Romanian, the number of young Christian adults was limited. When Faith became a young adult, she wanted to fellowship with other Christian men and women her age. She also wanted to be able to invite friends for whom she was burdened to church to hear the gospel in a language they could understand. She left the Romanian Baptist church and joined Grace Baptist Church in Akron, Ohio. She went to Kent State University for a year and then found employment as a legal secretary in downtown Akron.

A friend of hers enrolled in classes at Cornus Hill Bible College, and this friend invited Faith to attend classes with her. Partly to appease her friend, Faith began attending too. On one particular night in March of 1955, Faith needed transportation because of the distance between her office, the bus line, the college, and her home. She mentioned that need to another girl in one of her classes. This girl said she would ask the young man that drove her home if he would be willing to take Faith too. The young man that drove her was Roy Thompson. He consented to this request. Faith and Roy were complete strangers. Faith incorrectly assumed that the other girl and Roy were dating. She knew absolutely nothing about him. Larry had told Roy that "there was a pretty girl there who plays the piano at night," and this was the girl he was now driving home from class. When they crossed paths at a sandwich shop near the college, Faith had only ridden in the backseat of Roy's car; at that point, she only recognized him by the back of his head, but he recognized her!

Roy was still involved in holding services in various places with others from the college. Faith was asked to play the piano for this group and she agreed. One night, Roy was tasked with leading singing, which he had never done. Faith played a brief introduction to the hymn, which is what piano players almost always do. Roy was not expecting it and was frazzled. He didn't know when to start singing. He looked at Faith and snarled,

"Would you just play it the way it is on the page?"

Between the car rides home and the opportunities to minister together, their relationship warmed. They began attending services at Akron Baptist Temple together. Their first date was at a gospel singing where the Blackwood Brothers were featured. As the 1955 spring turned into summer, they became a steady couple. When they got to the point where he assumed they were going to get married, Faith said, "You know, you've never actually asked me to marry you." From that point on, he jokingly began telling people she proposed to him. On a Friday night in mid-July, they attended another singing event hosted by Dorothy and Ed. When it ended, Roy waited for all of the guests to leave. He used the moment of privacy to give Faith an engagement ring and request her hand in marriage. She accepted, and a wedding date was set for August of 1956, a little over a year down the road.

Roy and Larry were scheduled to leave for BBC six weeks later. The more Roy thought about the timetable that was set, the less he wanted to wait until August of '56 to be married. Before leaving for Springfield, he told Faith he wanted to get married in December of '55. She told him that she wasn't sure whether she'd be able to put a wedding together in just a few months, but he had confidence in her. She said she'd try. Faith later recalled, "Whether misplaced or not, he always had confidence in me."

When Roy arrived at BBC, he found himself surrounded by tremendously accomplished preachers and soulwinners. He had known all about Dallas Billington and B.R. Lakin, but he was introduced to G.B. Vick, Noel Smith, Bill Dowell, and others. In the fall of '55, BBC was in its sixth year of training preachers and missionaries to fulfill the Great Commission. There were 450 students. Its emphasis was on church planting. There was a pioneer spirit. Six years later, when future CBC staff member Bruce Musselman was there, the school's enrollment had grown to 850. The students were active in preaching and winning souls, because an emphasis was placed on service. As young people, Roy and Larry still managed to have fun. An unconfirmed legend persists that at one point a motorcycle was ridden into one of the halls on campus, and Roy Thompson may have been involved.

In addition to Larry, one of Roy's roommates was Ron Wolvin. Ron's parents died when he was three. He was raised by his grandmother in Detroit, Michigan, and worked in an auto factory after graduating from high school. He was a member of the church where G.B. Vick pastored. When God called him to preach, it was a natural fit that he would attend the college of which his pastor was president. The death of one of Ron's own brothers not long before he left for BBC caused him to forge a deep bond with his roommates. Their class had about 130 students upon entry, almost all of whom graduated. While Larry knew he was going to be an evangelist, God kept the city of Cleveland on Roy's mind throughout his time at BBC. The fact that God holds His men responsible for reaching their own generation was a notion that blazed profound determination into the heart of Roy Thompson.

Roy came home on Christmas break and pulled into Faith's driveway, out of gas and with 86 cents in his pocket. Faith's grandparents were not in favor of her marrying Roy. They thought all preachers were poor and that she wouldn't ever get to go anywhere or do anything. They wanted her to marry someone who shared their Romanian background and culture, and preferably someone of "means." But Faith knew it was God's will that she marry Roy Thompson. Larry had written her a letter from BBC saying that he was shipping Roy home because all he did was complain about how much he missed her. She knew how much he loved her.

With the help of friends, co-workers, and family, the couple married on December 23, 1955, at Grace Baptist Church. Not forsaking her childhood church, their reception was held at the Romanian Baptist church. Not surprisingly, the best man was Larry Clayton. The new husband and wife enjoyed a four-day honeymoon in Washington, D.C., courtesy of the Christmas bonus given to Faith by her boss.

In January, they headed to Springfield. Faith assumed that Roy had found a place for them to live, but Roy's "take no thought for the morrow" approach resulted in their two-day stay at a hotel upon arrival in Missouri. After they found a small apartment, Faith secured a job working as a secretary to a bank president. Roy worked at various jobs including pressing pants in a garment factory. This first year of their marriage brought many changes in their lives. Summer work was difficult to find in Springfield, so in May of 1956, Roy and Faith came home to Akron so Roy could find work while Faith was pregnant with their first child. When September rolled around again, the Thompson family was back in Springfield. Roy was back in school and working at the same time.

On October 28, 1956, their firstborn child, Joyce, was born. Roy felt it was important that Faith stay home with their newborn baby and found extra work to help make ends meet. This was a difficult time financially in their lives, but the Lord always provided.

It was during this time that Roy began his first pastorate. In their second year at BBC, Larry and Roy would hold street revivals in the towns and villages that surrounded Springfield.

One Saturday, several carloads of BBC students arrived in Nevada, Missouri, about 100 miles from Springfield. Those who worked the nearby farms would come into town on Saturdays, so there were people to whom the students could minister. Before beginning the revival, Larry found the sheriff to make him aware of the group's plans. He told him that they would use a loudspeaker, but it would not be excessive. He asked if there were places such as nursing homes or hospitals that should be left as undisturbed as possible.

The sheriff told him, "That doesn't matter, because you're not allowed to do this without my permission anyhow." Larry pointed to a nearby stop sign. At the bottom of the sign, there were empty whiskey bottles piled on the ground. They had been left there by the drunks who had been there the previous evening. Larry looked at the sheriff and said, "If you're not going to throw those whiskey bottles out, then you're not going to throw us out." With that, they were allowed to preach.

As the ministry went on, a gentleman across the street told them that if they really believed what they were preaching, he would be their first church member. He also told them he owned a rest home with a little chapel, and he'd be glad to let them use it for services. That conversation led to the inception of the Nevada Baptist Temple, of which Roy became pastor. The Thompson family, along with a few friends, would hop in Roy's '49 Ford and go to Nevada on Saturdays to visit and then remain for services on Sunday. Each week Roy brought his quick-witted, prank-loving roommate, Ron Wolvin, with him to lead the music, while Larry was out preaching everywhere he could.

By Roy's third and final year in Baptist Bible College, he had turned his church over to another student so he could concentrate on completing his studies while providing for his growing family. God blessed the Thompson family with a son, Mark David, who was born on December 30, 1957. In May of 1958, Roy graduated from Baptist Bible College as valedictorian of his class.

After graduation, Larry, Ron, and Roy went their separate ways. Larry went to Wichita where he had a two-week tent revival scheduled. In the first week of that meeting, 85 people attended. In the second week, it grew to 115. Another week was added because the crowd had grown to 300. He continued preaching all over Kansas that summer. Ron went to San Bernadino, California to plant a church.

The Thompson family went to Akron to stay with Faith's grandparents. After a couple weeks in Akron, according to Larry, "Roy got tired of it and wanted to go start a church." He still didn't know any preachers in Cleveland other than the one who had offered him a job, but that didn't faze him. On to Cleveland went the Thompsons, where Roy knew God wanted him to begin reaching needy souls with the eternity-changing message of Jesus Christ.

There was a spiritual wall around the city, and Roy Thompson planned to scale it.

Faith and Her Parents

Faith Sherban

Roy and Faith Thompson

Roy Thompson

Roy and Faith Thompson,
Mabel Thompson, and
Dorothy

Nevada Baptist Temple

CHAPTER FIVE

A Needy Place

*...assuredly gathering that the Lord had called us
for to preach the gospel to them.*—Acts 16:10

Upon their arrival in Cleveland, Roy and Faith, along with their two small children, moved into a small, bug-infested apartment at W. 45th and Marvin. That summer the temperature was hot, the humidity was high, and in 1958 there was no such luxury as central air conditioning. Roy found employment at Western Auto during the day and at the downtown post office on third shift. He would come home from the post office, sleep three hours, then get up to sell auto parts, all while still knocking on doors and trying to search out the neighborhood for a place to house a church. Eventually he was hired by Middle Atlantic Trucking to load trucks at night, which paid $125 a week, more than he'd ever made in his life.

Dr. Dallas Billington attempted to dissuade Roy about his choice of location to begin a church. Dr. Billington told him that many others had tried to start a Baptist church in the Cleveland area, without success. This was largely due to the fact that it was predominantly Catholic. Dr. Billington and other pastors came to dub Cleveland as "the graveyard of preachers," but Roy Thompson would not be dissuaded. He knew what city God was asking him to scale.

Occasionally, as the long, hot days dragged by, Roy was discouraged for lack of a place to meet. Finally, in the middle of summer, Roy spotted a house at 5614 Memphis Avenue that had a "For Sale" sign on it. It was about the 400th door he knocked on. Roy inquired about it and found out that a man who lived across the street owned it. He had told the current tenants that they could continue to rent it, but if he found a buyer, they would have to move out. They were prepared for this and began looking for another place to live in the event that their landlord found a buyer. When Roy asked the owner about the possibility of renting it with an option to eventually buy, he said, "Yes, but only if the current tenant is willing to move out." The family living in it at the time was that of Orlando Folger.

Pastor Thompson became increasingly excited as he walked through the house and saw potential opportunities for the church. The living room was large enough to be used for an auditorium. The bedrooms could be used for Sunday school classes. The kitchen could serve as a nursery. Even the closets provided usable space. The decision as to whether or not this house was going to be used for church services, however, belonged to Orlando Folger.

Orlando Folger was a Methodist, but he was saved. His son, Dick, was a Baptist and was in Bible college studying to become a preacher. Orlando realized that when Dick was ready to start a church, he might find himself in a similar position as Roy

Thompson. He sympathized. Another factor in his decision was that he had been looking for a place to move to in case the house sold. Not only did he agree to move out so the church could get started, but he was also eager to bring his own grown sons, daughters, and grandchildren to the services. Pastor Thompson later recalled, "I think it was a chance for him to do something for the Lord that he had never had a chance to do before." This was a day unlike any other day in the life of Roy Thompson. To him, it was a day of miracles.

Although Dr. Billington preferred that Roy begin a church elsewhere, he still promised him that Akron Baptist Temple would pay the church's rent for one year. Roy called Dr. Billington with the news that the house would be available, and the first service was scheduled for August 8th, 1958.

The wise man was scaling the city's wall.

House on Memphis Avenue

CHAPTER SIX

A Young Church

And some of them believed...—Acts 17:4

The church began with 12 people at the first service. In attendance were the four members of the Thompson family, Orlando Folger, two of his daughters, Fonda Folger, Miriam Folger Kaiser, her husband Vernon, and their two children. Pastor Thompson's mother and Faith Thompson's grandmother were also there for the first service. Folding chairs were placed in the living room and Pastor Thompson spoke from the area in front of the fireplace. As more people started attending, the dining room was filled with folding chairs as well.

Within the next couple weeks Orlando Folger's son Bob, and his wife, Nancy, came and visited the church along with their two young children, Brenda and Kevin. They came at the request of Bob's father, as did Carl "Skip" Folger, Orlando's other son, who was a teenager at the time. Bob and Nancy would later play a major role in the history and development of the church.

Nancy grew up in Sistersville, a small town in West Virginia and the same town where Orlando Folger was raised. At one point, Sistersville was booming, as oil seekers had struck gold. It was said that there were 10 millionaires there at one time. Coincidentally, Orlando had worked the oil fields with Nancy's grandfather years earlier.

Nancy was saved at Sistersville Baptist Church when she was 20 years old, the same year her father died of a heart attack. She met Bob at a camp in West Virginia. Bob and his twin brother, Dick, were visiting from Brooklyn, Ohio, where they lived. Bob and Nancy were introduced to one another through mutual friends and family. Bob had been saved as a teenager, and Nancy had gone to school with several of Bob's cousins.

Bob and Dick Folger entered the service in 1951. In light of their pleasant acquaintance, Nancy sent a birthday card to Bob in the state of Washington, where he and Dick were both stationed. They exchanged letters for the next two years. Bob proposed to her in a letter in December of 1953. He wrote, "I want to get you a ring for Christmas." He was released from the service, and in June of '54, they were married. Bob managed a produce department at a local grocery store until securing a higher-paying job as a truck driver. Their first child, Brenda, was born two years later. Their son, Kevin, arrived in 1957. He was nine months old when they began attending services at Cleveland Baptist Church.

This small nucleus of members was thrilled with its new church and preacher. Each one went away excited about going back for the next service. Bob was baptized after a couple months of attending because he had only been sprinkled. Before long, Nancy was staffing the nursery while Bob was teaching Sunday school. During the week, Bob would use index cards with Bible verses on them tucked into his windshield visor so he could memorize Scripture as he drove.

Larry and Roy stayed in touch after graduation. In October, Larry arrived in Cleveland to conduct the church's first revival meeting. He met Bob Folger for the first time and was impressed with how genuine he was. They had been working on persuading the neighbors to visit the church for the revival, and one of the little girls attended. When she got home, she told her mom that she met a truck driver who wasn't vulgar. Her mother didn't believe her. She said, "Oh yes, he taught my Sunday school class!" Her mom said she needed to see this for herself. When her mom attended, she got saved. Visitation became a group effort and the church began to grow.

One woman who was saved in that first revival was Dorothy Klotzsche. She had lived a partying lifestyle and had delivered a child at the age of 15. She began attending only a few weeks into the church's existence. Her boys had heard that there would be corn on the cob after the service, and she brought all nine of her children -- attendance doubled!

Dorothy's husband, Richard, joined them several months later. For about six months every time Richard heard a sermon, he did not want to believe it. He was German and had a Protestant background. He would go home and study the Bible to try to prove the preacher wrong. The more he read the Scriptures, the more he realized that "the word of the Lord is right" (Psalm 33:4). He understood the truth of Romans 3:4: "let God be true, but every man a liar." All he proved in his searching of the Scriptures (John 5:39, Acts 17:11) was that the preaching was correct because it was straight from the Bible. Upon recognition of this, Richard repented of his sin and asked Jesus Christ to save his soul. He poured out all the beer that he had and never bought or drank anymore of it the rest of his life. Twenty years after this first revival meeting, Dorothy's son, Bruce, would marry Joyce Thompson.

New converts were baptized at Parma Baptist Church. Pastor Thompson had been preaching on proper baptism, and his wife, Faith, was convicted by the Holy Spirit during these messages because she had not been correctly baptized. She was worried because she felt that if she admitted it, her husband's ministry might lose credibility. After all, she was not only the pastor's wife, but she also taught Sunday school and played the piano. She was troubled about it and couldn't sleep. One night, she tossed and turned until Roy was awakened. When she explained her dilemma, Roy said, "Why do you care what people think?" This motto of faithfulness to Christ despite people's opinions became a pattern for the Thompsons' ministry. Faith was baptized by her own husband shortly thereafter. By her example of humility and obedience to Christ, other converts submitted to proper baptism too. The church roll grew.

The strength of the confidence of mighty men was being cast down.

Bob and Dick Folger

Richard and Dorothy Klotzsche

Bob Folger

Bob and Nancy Folger

REVIVAL
• CRUSADE FOR SOULS •

CLEVELAND BAPTIST CHURCH
5614 Memphis Ave.

OCTOBER 12 thru 19 - NIGHTLY at 7:45 P.M.

SPEAKER: PASTOR:
Evangelist Larry Clayton   Roy Thompson

Flier From First Revival

CHAPTER SEVEN
An Exciting Time

From house to house, testifying...—Acts 20:20-21

By 1959, this industrious group of born-again, baptized believers had outgrown the house. It wasn't that there were too many people to fit into it. Rather, Dr. Billington had advised Roy that a church must have room to grow; there must be empty space that looks like it needs to be filled or else its people will fall prey to a sense of contentment with its current size. The task of finding a new location would be difficult because Pastor Thompson was still working a job in addition to pastoring the church.

Dr. Billington had paid the church's rent and provided chairs and songbooks from Akron Baptist Temple, but for the first year, he didn't provide financial support for Pastor Thompson. He wanted to see that young preachers were serious about their ministry before committing financial resources to them. After about a year, he offered to pay Pastor Thompson a salary, but the catch was that he'd have to quit his job at Middle Atlantic. More time would be freed up for ministry, but it would mean his income would decrease from $125 a week to $75 a week. Roy chose the spiritual over the physical and never regretted it.

On the home front, money was tight, food was scarce, and many times, Roy literally wondered where their next meal would come from. Due to financial instability, the Thompsons lived in 11 different homes during their first two years in Cleveland. One of the ladies in the church was an accomplished seamstress and made most of the clothes for the Thompson children. In similar ways God supplied all their needs, and they praised Him for His blessings.

Being a pastor's wife was a big adjustment for Faith. She felt unprepared for this role. While she had attended Bible college in Akron, her time in Springfield was spent raising babies, not learning in the classroom. She was shy. She had to learn how to work with people, but God is faithful to equip His servants with what they need to accomplish the tasks He has given them. Faith's case was no exception. With grace, poise, and diligence, she raised her family while simultaneously ministering to the women of CBC.

Roy began looking around for another place to meet, and again, the Lord blessed his efforts and provided a building which was once a skating rink and more recently, a theater. It was located at 4910 Memphis Avenue. The rent was $400 a month, which would be covered by Akron Baptist Temple for the first few months. In March of 1959, there were about 70 people in attendance at the first service in the theater building. The number of rodents was never tallied, but it may have exceeded the number of people. Rats were ushered outside so worshippers could be ushered inside. There were no Sunday school rooms, so Pastor Thompson and Bob Folger constructed some themselves. Even the projector room (from the building's days as a theater) was used for Sunday school. Larry Clayton returned to conduct the church's third revival.

Vernon Davis attended one of the revival services in which Larry Clayton was preaching. Vernon had been leading the music at another Baptist church that was led by a pastor who was not conducting himself or the church properly. After the service, Larry and Vernon met. It turned out that they both had family from Archburg, Tennessee. Vernon mentioned that there were also a number of families at his current church with roots in Archburg. Larry encouraged him to invite them to the revival meeting. Vernon shared with Larry that his position as music director might be in jeopardy, and Larry said, "Why don't you come join Roy?"

Larry testified not only to the burden Roy had for Cleveland, but also to his character. Larry told Vernon that he had known Roy for seven years, and he would trust Roy with his wife, children, and money. He told Vernon that even though Roy wasn't a southerner, he loved Jesus Christ with all his heart, and he was a great preacher and a great soulwinner. That conversation made a deep impact on Vernon, and he promised to return and to invite others. Vernon came back to hear Roy Thompson preach and was thoroughly impressed. The preaching was passionate, biblically sound, direct, clear, and convicting. He had found a new church home.

Many of the visitors who Vernon invited arrived and said, "This is exactly what we used to have and what we have been looking for." The people Vernon brought with him weren't people who were just saved and baptized. They were people who practiced tithing, singing, soulwinning, and attending church faithfully. Vernon became the first choir director of Cleveland Baptist Church. His wife, Bernice, was an example and role model to the ladies, including Faith Thompson. The songs Vernon is most remembered for are "Ship Ahoy," "How Great Thou Art," and "The Old Rugged Cross."

Because there was still six months left on the lease for the house, the Thompsons moved into it for that period of time. In fact, that's where Larry stayed when he preached the aforementioned revival. The apartment where the Thompsons had been living prior to moving into the house on Memphis Avenue left much to be desired. The house on Memphis, too, had its flaws. Its heating system did not work properly, and Faith was forced to boil water to give the children baths and do the laundry (which sometimes had to be done twice because the pipes were rusty and the rust would get into the water supply).

Although Dr. Billington had tried to discourage Pastor Thompson from starting his work in Cleveland, he kept his eye on what was happening. He came up from Akron to visit Pastor Thompson and to see the ministry for himself. He also had a proposition for the young pastor to consider. A small church in Youngstown, Ohio had come to the point where it had blueprints for a building which would seat 500 people. Its people were looking for a pastor to lead them. They were financially able to provide a lovely home for the pastor and his family and to buy him a new car. Dr. Billington set forth this proposal to Roy and asked him to give up his church in Cleveland and move to Youngstown. It was actually more of a demand than a request. Pastor Thompson was a young man and wanted nothing more than to please Dr. Billington since he had been saved in his church and Akron Baptist Temple had been so helpful to the Cleveland ministry.

Pastor Thompson thought over the request for a couple of days. He looked around and saw what he had: a small, but growing church, a wife and two children that he could barely support, and a beat up old car. As tempting as it was to have a nice church building, a home for his family, financial security, and a new car, something didn't feel quite right to him. He knew God had called him to Cleveland, and he couldn't leave -- no matter what. Although Dr. Billington would have preferred Pastor Thompson move to Youngstown, he was secretly pleased that the young pastor showed determination to stay where he felt God had called him. Roy knew in his heart of hearts that he had to obey God and stay true to his calling, even if it meant displeasing a man he had come to love and admire.

Ultimately, it was Larry Clayton who became the pastor of the church in Youngstown. He pastored it for four years while still holding revival meetings throughout the country. He planted a church in western Ohio as well as one in Pittsburgh, Pennsylvania during the four years he pastored the church in Youngstown. He would later reside in Cleveland with his family and transfer his membership to Cleveland Baptist. He was in attendance whenever he was home, though he spent most of each year holding meetings all over the world.

The wise man didn't scale the city to leave it. He scaled it to reach its mighty men, many of whom hadn't yet placed their confidence in Christ.

Theater Building

Roy, Joyce, and Mark Thompson

Thompson Family

Pastor Thompson and Vernon Davis

CHAPTER EIGHT
A Larger Vision

Where there is no vision, the people perish. —
Proverbs 29:18

The 1960s brought many changes for Cleveland Baptist Church. By 1960, the ever-growing church was bursting at the seams in the theater building. In just two years, the small nucleus had grown into a membership of 100. Joe and Phyllis Wilson were in charge of the youth department while Vernon Davis brought a godly spirit and a God-honoring approach to the music ministry. Bob Folger was willing to do anything that needed to be done -- he remodeled; he taught; he cleaned; he fixed anything that was broken; he knocked on doors; he fixed automobiles. He and Nancy picked up teenagers and children for church, and they had other church members over for dinner. These early pillars of CBC allowed their love for God to govern their everyday lives. Their love for Him translated to a love for people. They didn't ask, "Why do we have to do this?" or "Why are we not allowed to go here?" They claimed Mark 8:35, which says, "whosoever shall lose his life for my sake and the gospel's, the same shall save it."

It was during this time of growth that Pastor Thompson approached his congregation about the possibility of securing property to construct a permanent building to house the church. Some of the members were a little concerned regarding the financing of such a project. The church was already supporting two missionaries out of its already tight budget; how could it afford its own property, let alone a building? The pastor then told the people that there was a wealthy man in Dr. Billington's church by the name of James Lawson, who owned the Lawson Milk Company and its stores in the surrounding areas. He had set up a trust fund with $500,000 for the sole purpose of helping establish new Baptist churches. This money would be loaned to new churches with no interest required. Cleveland Baptist Church received a loan of $125,000 to buy property. This was truly a "deal" that the church could not afford to turn down.

With that knowledge in mind, Pastor Thompson and some of the members began looking for property upon which to build a church house. He went to the Mayor of Brooklyn, John M. Coyne, to make him aware of the church's plans. Mayor Coyne liked that Pastor Thompson had consulted him. It flattered him, and the two men developed a friendship. It was a wise relationship to build because politicians can either significantly help a cause, or severely hurt it. Pastor Thompson understood this and gained the mayor's support without compromising. He told Mayor Coyne that he was considering building at the bottom of the hill on Memphis Avenue, which, more than 50 years later, is an apartment complex adjacent to a field owned by the church. The mayor told him that it would be very difficult to get cars in and out of that area during the winter, and he recommended building on the plot of land on Tiedeman Road.

Mayor Coyne's suggestion was heeded and was, indeed, a helpful one. Seven acres of property were purchased. Mayor Coyne would go on to enjoy the longest consecutive tenure as mayor in United States history. In 2012, at the age of 96, he said, "The Cleveland Baptist Church was the best thing that ever happened to Brooklyn, Ohio."

Pastor Thompson contacted Dr. Billington, and he was pleased to be able to help out again. The floor plans were the same ones that were used for the Youngstown building. It would be virtually the same type of building that was constructed there and would seat 500 people. Groundbreaking was scheduled for September 4th, 1960. Bob Folger was going to turn the first shovel, but he ended up at the hospital instead. His and Nancy's third child, Vicky, arrived that day.

The church continued to meet in the theater building while the construction of the building on Tiedeman was in progress. Bob Folger spent his days driving a truck and his evenings at the construction site. A host of CBC men sacrificed their evenings in the same way. The final sermon in the theater building was delivered by none other than Larry Clayton. He recalled that the theme of his message was, "Moving on and moving up." He told them that churches grow one step at a time. He made an appeal to those who had a vision for the next level.

The builders worked hard to get the building ready for its debut. The men of the church laid the floor tile in the auditorium the Friday night before opening Sunday. They worked and worked and finally it was done, or so they thought. One of the men came back on Saturday to look things over, and he couldn't believe his eyes! The cold temperature of the night before had caused the tiles to buckle and pop out. All the work had to be redone. The men came back and worked the rest of Saturday and all through the night in order to have the auditorium ready for the morning service. Their diligence paid off, and the floor was completed just before sunrise.

On Palm Sunday in 1961, Cleveland Baptist Church held its first service in its very own new building. Everyone in the church worked hard at visitation. They wanted the first service in the new building to be an exciting and memorable one, and indeed it was. The people kept coming. Every door was filled with people trying to get in. When the final count was taken, the total number in attendance was 425. Considering the new building seated 500, the auditorium was quite full.

In what is now the Bob Folger Fellowship Hall, there was an electrifying atmosphere. Anticipation of God's blessing was in the air, and the people were not to be disappointed. Pastor Thompson had planned to preach a sermon that he had prepared, but after the soloist sang "The Old Rugged Cross," Rev. Thompson knew that he couldn't preach the sermon he had planned. The Holy Spirit anointed him with a special grace that morning, and as he approached his brand new pulpit for the first time, he had everyone open their Bibles to Galatians 2:20: "I am crucified with Christ: nevertheless I live; yet not I, but Christ liveth in me: and the life which I now live in the flesh I live by the faith of the Son of God, who loved me, and gave himself for me."

The love of God was something that Roy Thompson knew about firsthand. If the love of God could reach him, then the love of God could reach anyone. That morning in 1961 the reality of the love of God touched the hearts of those in attendance and

42 men, women, and children came to know the Lord as their personal Savior.

The wise man showed them the One in whom the strength of their confidence should be.

New Building Construction

New Location

CHAPTER NINE

A Unique Collection

*Go out into the highways and hedges, and compel
them to come in, that my house may be filled.—*
Luke 14:23

While Pastor Thompson had an intense burden for the souls of men, he was also determined to maintain a Christ-honoring reputation in every area of ministry. James Lawson gave loans to other Baptist churches, many of which never repaid them. Pastor Thompson believed that God blesses an honest testimony. He also understood that if churches didn't pay their loans back, the opportunity for more churches to receive loans would be limited. The more loans were paid off, the more could be given out. Cleveland Baptist Church paid off every cent.

The first full-time staff member was hired the same year the church transitioned from the theater building to the property on Tiedeman. This was a young man who had known both Roy Thompson and Larry Clayton since 1955. His name was Ron Wolvin. They stayed in touch while he was busy in California.

While at BBC, they had talked about Ron coming to Cleveland to work with Roy someday, and though Pastor Thompson had a tremendous music director in Vernon Davis, he still saw value in making Ron part of the staff. Ron agreed to become Pastor Thompson's assistant, but said that he did not have the resources to get to Cleveland. Pastor Thompson told Ron he'd give him a credit card to pay for the gas that Ron's extra large Pontiac would require to make the cross-country trip.

According to Larry Clayton, Ron Wolvin was a "city boy." He wasn't as well-versed in loading trailers as "country folk." With the heaviest of luggage in the back of the trailer instead of the front, Ron's trip was not off to a good start. His wife, Geraldine, was expecting. They had nearly 2,000 miles to cover. His trailer was swinging violently from side to side. The Wolvins, however, survived the trek. When they arrived, the tone for Ron's time at CBC was set with a clever stunt that some would say epitomized him. In the middle of the night and about a half mile from Pastor Thompson's house, Ron pulled over to use a pay phone. He called Roy and said, "I'm out here in Wyoming and there's a preacher here that really needs an assistant. I've decided to take the job. I know I've put a lot of money on your credit card. I might pay you back someday."

Pastor Thompson disguised his frustration and said, "Well, if that's what you feel the Lord wants you to do, then you go ahead." He hung up the phone and said, "That crook!" Ron waited a few minutes, until he figured Roy would be back in bed. He pulled into the driveway, honked the horn, and knocked on the door. When Pastor Thompson opened the door, he shouted "Surprise!"

Cleveland Baptist had yet another character on its hands with Ron Wolvin on staff. Pastor Thompson enjoyed poking fun at Ron's height (or lack thereof). On one occasion he invited Ron to the platform to sing and made sure to adjust the microphone to a height of about three feet. Ron responded by comparing the length of the microphone to Pastor Thompson's nose. Moments like these brought levity and entertainment to a thriving church.

A problem arose in 1963, after the completion of the first addition to the building. The church had just built the current HBI chapel and its surrounding classrooms. Brooklyn's fire chief continually nitpicked about a particular building code stipulation. Unfortunately, the project was finished before this loophole could be addressed. The decision Pastor Thompson had made to treat Mayor Coyne with respect and reverence paid off. Mayor Coyne called a meeting at City Hall, and he invited Pastor Thompson to attend. He told his staff, "You are not to bother this church or this pastor." That issue was settled.

As the '60s marched on, Cleveland Baptist Church continued to grow. By 1964, there were more than 600 people attending services. The church's booming growth can be explained by a number of factors. It had the hand of God upon it because it was faithful to soulwinning. It had a dynamic preacher. There were very few, if any, other evangelistic-minded churches in the area. It also had Ron Wolvin leading singing. He was a people person. He was enthusiastic. He and Roy were a good team on the platform. They made people feel like church was an exciting place to be. Not only did the church grow, but so did the Thompson family. Ruth Elizabeth Thompson made her way into the world on Sunday morning, February 2, 1964.

Among the children of the church in the mid '60s were future pastors such as Kevin Folger, Dan Wolvin, and the Clayton boys, Steve and Phil. They grew up observing a flourishing ministry, as did Joyce and Mark Thompson and others. The boys begged their dads to bring them to work with them in the summer so they could play on the mounds of dirt while the new auditorium was being built and explore along the creek. Dan Wolvin recalls his childhood days when the invitations were given on Sunday mornings: "One of my greatest memories was counting the people who got saved. We would hold up one finger for each person. It sometimes took three or four of us to count them all."

Pastor Thompson enjoyed his church and his people and became a regular at the activities of all the various Sunday school departments. There were "get acquainted" activities, picnics, and Saturday night gospel sings. Many times he was the entertainment since he was able to act out various roles, especially in the area of comedy.

One Sunday, immediately following the morning service, Pastor Thompson and Larry Clayton left for Jacksonville, Florida, to attend a fellowship meeting. It was a 24-hour drive because I-75 was not yet built. The roads were narrow, and they cut through the mountains, making it difficult for a vehicle to pick up speed. When they made it into the mountains of the Carolinas, they turned on the radio. They found a broadcast of a sermon about heaven being preached by John Rawlings. He carefully described what the Bible says happens to those who belong to Jesus when they are with their Savior.

Roy and Larry, two God-called preachers, were blessed and moved as they listened. They began weeping. Roy had to pull the car off to the side of the road. They wept with their heads against the dashboard and praised the Lord of glory for His marvelous, redemptive grace. This was the deep, abiding love for the Lord Jesus upon which Cleveland Baptist Church was built. It wasn't built on gimmicks or advertisements. It wasn't built on bells and whistles. Roy Thompson, Larry Clayton, Ron Wolvin, Bob Folger, and their families and friends simply desired that the Lamb of God receive the preeminence that He is due. That is why God blessed this church.

Ron Wolvin

Thompson family

New Addition

A Diligent Mindset

*Deliver the poor and needy; rid them out of the
hand of the wicked.*—Psalm 82:4

By 1968, Bob Folger was the director of the youth
department. He would take teenagers out on visitation
and have them over to his house. He and his wife would
give anything to make a spiritual imprint on their lives. Sometimes
young people would visit the Folgers' house on Saturday nights
and never go home before the service the next morning. Bob
and Nancy piled teenagers into their car for church until they
could not fit another person.

With no Christian school in operation at the time, the youth
of CBC attended schools like West Tech and John Marshall.
Many of them invited friends from school and friends from their
neighborhoods to church. On one occasion, a young man had
surrendered for full-time ministry and had decided to go to BBC.
He didn't have a car, so Bob let him borrow his car. This young
man went to Missouri and proceeded to sell the car. Bob never

got a dime from him, but he believed Philippians 3:8, "…I count all things but loss for the excellency of the knowledge of Christ Jesus my Lord."

Bob had been a truck driver for over a decade and all of his work for the church was voluntary. One day, his job took him to Vermilion, Ohio. He stepped out of his truck and his foot inadvertently landed on a golf ball. He was badly injured. He was in the hospital for three weeks with intense pain. To make matters worse, he had a doctor who handled the incident in a most unprofessional way. His office was dirty, unorganized, and he performed a procedure with an instrument that hadn't been cleaned properly, complicating Bob's condition. Bob was in a cast for almost a year. He had to keep his leg as still as possible or the discomfort would escalate.

Bob's being out of work for a year took a financial toll on the Folger household. Then the opportunity to receive compensation came. There was a hearing to determine the specifics of what had taken place. When questioned about the care provided, the doctor's incompetence was apparent. Due to his disheveled records, he failed to correctly identify which leg he had treated. For years prior to the injury, Pastor Thompson had been asking Bob to join the church staff full-time. Bob had been reluctant because he wasn't sure he could support his family on an associate pastor's salary. Bob realized that this ordeal was God's way of teaching him to trust Him for provision. It was also God's way of directing him away from truck driving and toward the staff of Cleveland Baptist Church.

Upon his recovery, Bob joined the church staff in 1969, and the timing was perfect. Just as Akron Baptist Temple had been doing, the Lord led Pastor Thompson to begin a bus ministry.

Bob's well-roundedness and hard-working spirit compelled him to be involved in almost everything CBC did, but the bus ministry captured his heart. He knew how automobiles worked, and his experience as a truck driver proved beneficial. When the bus ministry first started, there was no bus garage, but Bob still worked on buses in the snow and rain. The church could not afford the finest parts or the finest buses, but it had a man determined to keep them on the road. Larry Clayton made a sign addressing the bus parts scattered throughout the parking lot as "Bob Folger's Junkyard."

Instead of trying to fit as many kids into cars as possible, the church could now provide transportation for anyone. This eliminated another excuse for those invited to services to decline, and it increased church attendance dramatically. Among the men who God used in the early days of this ministry were Ken Williams, Garth Hulin, Dick Reffitt, Jerry Nolan and countless others. This ministry would provide opportunities to train young people to serve God. It would get more souls under the sound of the gospel. It would be used of God to pick men up "out of the miry clay" and set their "feet upon a rock" (Psalm 40:2). Future pastors, Sunday school teachers, soulwinners, missionaries, and servants of Jesus Christ would be reached through Cleveland Baptist Church's willingness to buy and use buses. In 1970, a garage was built to allow repairs and maintenance to be handled in-house.

Roy Thompson had a life insurance policy on himself. The sum that he and the church had paid into it was significant. When the bus fleet needed to be updated, Pastor Thompson went to the bank, cashed in the policy, and bought buses. That's who Roy Thompson was. He was a spontaneous risk taker. When the risks that he took worked out, it was usually for the good of the gospel of Jesus Christ. Decisions like that, which go unheralded by the world, represented the heart and burden of a selfless servant who wished that Jesus Christ would be exalted. The bus fleet would grow to include more than 15 buses. The number of individuals who received the free gift of eternal life after riding a bus to Cleveland Baptist Church is a number known only to God, but it is indeed a large one.

When the first auditorium on Tiedeman Road was built, the church had about 100 members. Adding space to seat 500 seemed presumptuous to some, but it filled quickly; seven years later, 500 seats were not enough. Another building was needed. Attendance soared when the bus ministry launched. Door-knocking and other outreach programs met with exponential success. This time a much larger auditorium would be built adjacent to the first one.

The church broke ground on the new auditorium in 1968, and it was completed the following year. Its architecture and design were modern, and it reflected the contemporary style of its day. The balcony was initially divided and used for Sunday school. In 11 years, Cleveland Baptist Church had gone from meeting in a living room to meeting in a 1,500-seat auditorium. The church went through four building programs. Though nobody spoke openly about it, some of the core families mortgaged their homes to support the building of the new auditorium. They understood that people must sacrifice in order to accomplish something extraordinary. They wanted Cleveland Baptist to do something extraordinary for Jesus Christ.

Visitors learned that church can be fun. Jim Jones Sr., who began attending in 1968, noticed the way Pastor Thompson, Ron

Wolvin, Bob Folger, and Larry Clayton poked fun at one another. He enjoyed the laughter and the family atmosphere. There was a sense of playfulness that balanced the intensity and tenderness of the sermons that were delivered. Members wanted to invite lost friends and family members to be part of this special church.

On a snowy winter day in 1969, the four men were on their way to a church on the east side of Cleveland. Bob was driving, with Roy in the passenger seat and Ron and Larry in the backseat. As Bob was driving, Ron began to flick his ears. Ron could flick an ear with surprising force. Bob's ears were getting "redder than blood," according to Larry. With his hands occupied, Bob was forced to endure this affliction. He said, "That's okay, Ron, I won't always be driving." Ron stated smugly that for the moment, he was driving, and there was nothing he could do about it. Tension was building. Bob was larger than Ron. Bob preferred that iniquity not go unpunished. Ron was getting nervous as the trip was winding down.

When the men arrived at the parking lot of their destination, Ron knew his consequences were only moments away. As soon as the car was in park, he opened the door and ran. Bob chased him and quickly closed in on him. Seconds later, Ron, dressed in a suit and tie, was sticking feet-first out of a massive snow drift. Pastor Thompson said, "Serves him right!" as he and Bob nonchalantly entered the building, leaving Larry to dig Ron out. This episode, along with countless others like it, typified the sense of humor and unforgettable camaraderie in the early days of something special that God was doing in a city that had been scaled.

Bob Folger

Groundbreaking for New Auditorium

New Auditorium Construction

New Auditorium

CBC Bus

Jones Family

CHAPTER ELEVEN

A Stand Taken

*Who will rise up for me against the evildoers? or
who will stand up for me against the workers of
iniquity?*—Psalm 94:16

During the first decade or so of his ministry as pastor of Cleveland Baptist Church, Roy Thompson was a guest speaker in many churches and at revivals throughout the country. He became widely known for his stand on moral and political issues of the day. He strongly and publicly opposed pornography, unclean textbooks in the public schools, and abortion. Not only was he firm on political issues, but he also took a stance when he felt someone in the ministry was using Cleveland Baptist or any other church to compromise the teachings of Christ.

One such man, in Pastor Thompson's opinion, was Bob Harrington, also known as "The Chaplin of Bourbon Street." This man purportedly had a ministry on the streets and in the bars of New Orleans. He had written a book which had become popular in Baptist circles; many fundamental preachers were even having him preach in their pulpits. Once Pastor Thompson read his book, *The Chaplin of Bourbon Street*, he became the only fundamental, Bible-believing preacher who refused to have anything to do with Bob Harrington. He was infuriated by what he read because God's name was blatantly taken in vain, vulgar and obscene words were frequently used, and it was stated that the confessional booth was a place of salvation.

A Baptist Bible Fellowship meeting in Virginia was planned for the purpose of electing new officers. Pastor Thompson had been nominated to become president of the fellowship. Because of this nomination, he was the featured speaker of the meeting. This event coincided with the peak of Bob Harrington's "career" in fundamental churches. Roy Thompson stood up with a copy of the book in hand, read some of the heretical teachings from it, spat on it, threw it across the platform, and stated, "Be it known that the Cleveland Baptist Church has no fellowship with the churches or pastors who endorse this." With that statement, he walked off the platform, took Mrs. Thompson from the audience, and left. His stand on this issue cost him the coveted position of president of the fellowship. Even though his "performance" caused some shock waves that evening, in time, the preachers in that meeting came to acknowledge that his characterization of Bob Harrington was, indeed, accurate.

Discerning which associations honored Christ and which ones did not was not the only challenge Pastor Thompson faced. Around him, the moral fiber of America was crumbling. Though Cleveland Baptist Church remained committed to godliness in the 1960s, America as a whole did not. Drugs, alcohol, rock-and-roll music, and rampant adultery became staples of the Baby Boomer generation. Hippies protested the Vietnam War as patriotism sank to an all-time low. College students denounced the American military as "murderers" but didn't seem to mind the atrocities committed by the Communist Vietcong against the innocent villagers of South Vietnam.

Pacifism took root as multitudes naively concluded that liberty was not worth fighting for. "If it feels good, do it" was the motto of the day. The rejection of universal truth resulted in the pursuit of hedonistic pleasure. Right and wrong were replaced with what was preferred by the individual. Prayer and Bible reading had been banned in public schools since the early '60s.

In 1973, the Supreme Court sided with a Texas woman named Norma McCorvey in a case that legally sanctioned bloodshed. She was denied an abortion and argued that being forbidden by law to murder her baby was unconstitutional. In a 7-2 decision, *Roe v. Wade* provided for legal abortions in all 50 states. Amidst this moral crisis in America, battle lines were drawn, and Roy Thompson was spiritually entrenched.

While Joyce Thompson was a student at Midpark High School, she asked her mom to get a book for her because it was required reading in her English class. Faith obtained the book and began reading it. She was shocked and appalled at the sinfulness of its contents. She called her husband and told him what Joyce was assigned to read. When Pastor Thompson came home, he read the book and was disgusted and outraged. He called the school and made an appointment with the English teacher and the principal. He told them, "She is not going to read that book and you are not going to fail her." They belittled him and suggested that he was not educated enough to appreciate it. The culture of the public school was worsening. The incident caused Roy to begin seriously considering opening a Christian school.

People respect a leader with a willingness to admit his mistakes. People can relate to one who realizes he is not perfect. Roy Thompson was willing to admit when he was wrong. For years, he had said that Cleveland Baptist Church would not have a Christian school. He had said that to start one would be to take the light of Christ out of the public schools. By the fall of 1974, he was finished tolerating the humanistic indoctrination of the public schools. The schools presented evolution not as a theory, but as fact. They taught that all religions are equally valid, contradicting the exclusive claims of Christ. Pastor Thompson realized that without a Christian school, the church would have no kids left.

Joyce and Mark Thompson and Brenda Folger had already graduated, but Ruthy Thompson had some schooling yet to finish. Joyce, who would go to BBC in 1974, and Mark were enrolled in a program that allowed them to earn credits early enough to graduate at age 16, but there were enough young people, including Kevin and Vicky Folger, who would appreciate the opportunity to attend a Christian school.

Talk of opening a school was considered, and talk became action. Pastor Thompson had always believed in doing what needed to be done and sorting out the details later. God touched his heart about the need. He spoke with parents who sensed the same direction from the Lord. Heritage Christian School opened just months after the initial discussions about it. In its first year, there were about 160 students meeting in the church building. The principal was Stan Knisley, a Bob Jones University graduate. He and his wife had been members of Canton Baptist

Temple. Most of the teachers Stan hired were fellow Bob Jones graduates. The juniors and seniors were proud and excited to be pioneers in this new form of education. Kevin Folger was among the six students of the first senior class. Fittingly, Larry Clayton preached the first chapel service. Bob Folger and B.R. Lakin would also preach chapel services that year. By its second year, HCS had more than 300 students enrolled.

Heritage Christian School opened at a time when other Bible-believing churches were encountering the same challenges. A statewide organization known as Christian Schools of Ohio and a national organization known as the Christian Law Association were born. CLA was founded by David Gibbs, a member of Cleveland Baptist at the time. Pastor Thompson became President of both organizations. There were countless other Baptist preachers who could have taken the lead in fighting for this cause, but Roy Thompson's passion was unsurpassed. It was natural that he would be at the front of the battle. When Christian schools became a perceived threat to the Ohio Board of Education, the Board wanted to close them, stating that they did not meet the minimum standards for education. In Canal Winchester, Ohio, children were forcefully taken from their parents because the state said the children were truant for not attending a state-certified school.

Pastor Thompson and David Gibbs garnered support for the cause of Christian education. Several small rallies were held for the purpose of building a big rally in Columbus to promote separation of church and state. Bob Folger did the leg work on the organization and logistics while Pastor Thompson spoke convincingly across the country. He rightly charged that the government was trying to control America's children instead of parents controlling their own children.

The big rally took place on a Monday when the legislators were not meeting. There were more than 100 bus loads of people in attendance that included 800 preachers and about 10,000 supporters. An article written in the Sunday "Plain Dealer Magazine" on April 25, 1976, stated that "Rev. Thompson led a victorious crusade in Columbus for the right of Christian schools to operate." Ohio's governor, James A. Rhodes, had been invited but no confirmation that he would be present was given. It made for extra drama when he arrived and publicly stated that "Christian schools are the last bastion of discipline left in the school system."

Another reporter with the Akron Beacon Journal wrote an article on this same rally. Dated September 14, 1975, the reporter wrote, "Despite the emotionalism of the rally, the group probably will not be able to achieve its goal overnight, if at all." One such goal that Pastor Thompson wanted to attain was a separate set of minimum standards for Christian schools. Ohio's school superintendent said "there was no reason for this" [a separate set of standards] and gave the impression that there would be no change. Thanks to Pastor Thompson's leadership, Christian schools have their own set of standards under which to operate today.

At one point, Pastor Thompson went down to the School Board and demanded that the superintendent be fired. He wasn't dismissed at the time, but he was dismissed three months later. The issue was not limited to the state of Ohio. In the midst of this saga, Pastor Thompson traveled to New Hampshire where a similar scenario was unfolding. A pastor there had opened a

Christian school and there was talk of his arrest. When Pastor Thompson got there, he told state officials, "If you arrest him, I'll be there the next day to open the school myself!" Soon other public figures echoed his statement by saying, "And if you arrest Roy Thompson, I'll be there to open it the day after that!" The pastor's boldness was inspiring.

The events leading to the arrival of another important figure in the history of Heritage Christian School began in 1968. Dorothy Klotzsche's son, Bruce Witzke, had grown up at Cleveland Baptist Church. The year Bruce was born his mother had married Richard Klotzsche. Bruce was just a boy when his mother and Richard were saved. He was part of the youth department of Cleveland Baptist all the way through his senior year at Strongsville High School. In fact, at age 18, Bruce was chosen as president of the youth group, however, he knew he wasn't saved. He quit going to church because he felt he couldn't lead a youth department as a lost young man. Bob Folger had known him for years, so Bob assumed the explanation for Bruce's absence was that he had just gotten upset with someone.

Bruce was a wrestler in high school and college and got mixed up with the wrong crowd when he stopped attending church. He started drinking. Over the next eight years, he became a truck driver with a dirty mouth and a penchant for bars. In the fall of 1976, at age 26, he and about 40 friends took a trip to the Mohican River in Loudonville, Ohio, to go canoeing. Bruce and a friend looked for a place to put their canoe in the water. They noticed a sign that read, "Do not go beyond this point," but they ignored it. They put their canoe in the river, climbed in, and before long it found troublesome waters. The current was strong. They were headed toward a waterfall. Bruce fell out of the canoe, and struggled against the current. With all of his might, he fought for a breath of air. Twice more he was able to get his mouth out of the water before getting sucked back down. He thought, "I can't keep fighting this! I'm going to die, and I'm going to wake up in hell." Somehow he surfaced and said to his friends, "I can't believe I'm not in hell." They had no idea what he was talking about.

About a month later, two of Cleveland Baptist's college students came by his house to visit his brother, who was not home. Bruce told them that he had grown up in that church, so they invited him to return. He went back to Cleveland Baptist Church the next Sunday and sat in the balcony. During the message he was under intense conviction, but he didn't respond. He went back to his job driving a truck. All week, he thought, "God is going to kill me. If He lets me live until Sunday, I'll get saved." He made it to the following Sunday, and this time he responded to the invitation. Bob Folger met him at the altar and led him to Christ. He never sat on another bar stool because he had become a new creature in Christ.

Bruce began reading the Scriptures and going on visitation. Over the next couple years he worked a bus route, got involved in ministry, and watched as God transformed his life. He married Joyce Thompson in 1978. Stan Knisley offered him and Joyce jobs teaching at Heritage. They began teaching the Monday following their wedding, joining the staff the same year Dave Cook did. The school's enrollment was so large it operated in two shifts in the church building. Bruce found a soulwinning partner in fellow teacher Ron Nelson, who had been hired a year earlier. Ron Nelson was a geologist with a master's degree who had gotten saved in Nevada. He had read in an advertisement that HCS was looking for a science teacher. He was offered the job over the phone, never having met Pastor Thompson face-to-face.

At one point, the school had more than 700 students because it was open to all denominations. Buses ran every morning to pick children up for school. Unfortunately, doctrinal differences began to create strife. Eventually, Stan Knisley sensed the Lord calling him to pastor a church in Bridgeport, West Virginia. At that time Pastor Thompson tightened the reins on the school and doctrinally purged it, decreasing its enrollment to less than 400.

Pastor Thompson also saw the need of higher education for the people of CBC and like-minded churches. In 1974, to help train servants of Christ, Heritage Baptist Institute was founded. Over the years, not only has it successfully produced scores of Sunday school teachers, but it has also graduated men who have become pastors, evangelists, and missionaries.

The very first of HBI's current 100 graduates was Gene Piazza, who went on to become the third pastor of Bedford Baptist Church, following Bruce Musselman and Larry Clayton. Many other graduates enjoyed stellar success in the ministry as well. Andy Rusnacko has pastored Bible Baptist Temple in Euclid for 34 years. Wolf Maldoff pastored Lakeland Baptist Temple in Eastlake for 20 years. Jessie Jones pastors Southeast Baptist Church on the east side of Cleveland. Jim Pranger has planted churches in Romania and Hungary. Greg Davis and John Lutz, both graduates of HBI, served at Cleveland Baptist, and went on to pastor churches in Northeast Ohio. Pastor Thompson felt that if he wasn't training people for the harvest field, then he wasn't doing his job.

Because of his involvement in the furtherance of the gospel and his role in Christian education, Bob Jones University believed that Rev. Roy Thompson had earned yet another degree. He had held an honorary doctorate from Midwestern Schools of Pontiac, Michigan since 1969, but in a ceremony on the campus of Bob Jones University in Greenville, South Carolina in May of 1978, he received another. Dr. Bob Jones, Sr., Chancellor of Bob Jones University, and his son, Dr. Bob Jones III, awarded Pastor Thompson the coveted degree. Over the years, other universities and colleges would also award him this special degree. Dr. Thompson, by the grace and blessings of God, had come a long way from his early childhood of poverty and shame.

In 1979, the religion editor of The Cleveland Press was making his rounds to different churches in the greater Cleveland area for a series of articles regarding the best preaching he heard during that time period. George R. Plagenz, after visiting 50 churches, presented the "Halo" award to Roy Thompson for preaching the best sermon of the 50 that he had heard. In addition, he gave the church his "five-star award" for its music. Once again, that great old hymn "The Old Rugged Cross," sung as a duet that morning, touched Mr. Plagenz' heart. He wrote:

> Whenever I have felt in need of inspiration, I have gone to one of two churches – Old Stone or Cleveland Baptist. It would take a psychiatrist to make sense out of that. The two churches – one liberal and the other rock-ribbed fundamentalist – have practically nothing in common. And while Dr. Lewis Raymond (at Old Stone) and I are close friends, I am not sure Rev. Roy Thompson at Cleveland Baptist even likes me – although I like

him. He would consider me a secular humanist. Maybe I like him because we both tend to be dogmatic. And we are both scolders.

These observations are indicative of a Bible-believing man of God who refused to back down, refused to compromise, and always pointed people to the Word of God.

There will always be men in a city who reject wisdom and prefer their own might. The wise man does not agree with their perceived strength; he casts it down.

A fundamentalist David takes aim

The Rev. Roy Thompson of Cleveland Baptist is foursquare for old-fashioned discipline and virtues

Columbus Rally

12—A   THE PLAIN DEALER, TUESDAY, DECEMBER 9, 1975

Rallying Baptists cheer Rhodes; he lauds their schools

By George E. Condon Jr.
Plain Dealer Special

COLUMBUS—Gov. James A. Rhodes drew the prayers and cheers of more than 8,000 fundamentalist Baptists yesterday when he pledged support of their efforts to keep their Bible-oriented schools open throughout the state.

Rhodes, his remarks often punctuated with shouts of "Amen" from the crowd gathered on the Statehouse lawn, declared, "A church school is the last bastion of discipline in our school system. I fully support the right of every parent in Ohio to send his children to a religiously centered school."

Yesterday's rally, the largest at the Statehouse in at least five years, was organized by Christian Schools of Ohio, a statewide organization of fundamentalists with headquarters in Cleveland.

It was designed to call attention to the plight of preachers swept up in recent efforts by prosecutors to close church schools for allegedly failing to measure up to state standards.

Rhodes said he would support legislation to establish separate standards for private schools. Such a bill will soon be introduced by State Sen. Anthony J. Celebrezze Jr., D-25, leaders of yesterday's rally said.

Court actions brought against ministers in Greenville in Darke County and in Canal Winchester, a Columbus suburb, were based on the failure of church schools to conform to all standards set by the Department of Education.

The Darke County case is pending in the Ohio Supreme Court. The Canal Winchester suit was dropped.

Yesterday's crowd, ranging from infants to the elderly, came to the Statehouse in a colorful procession of 145 buses emblazoned with the names of Baptist churches and schools across the state.

For more than an hour before the 1 p.m. rally began, protesters, some carrying Bibles and others waving flags, left the buses and joined the growing throng to sing hymns and patriotic songs.

Before the buses had emptied, Rhodes made his unexpected appearance on the Statehouse steps.

"This is what we need more of in Ohio—people coming forth publicly and pledging their right to worship God," Rhodes shouted.

"You are here because you believe in America, you believe in Ohio and you believe in God," he declared. "You're asking nothing more than to be left alone. God bless you in this fight. You can win because you're right."

After his speech, the crowd prayed for the governor.

Other speakers characterized the state's public school system as a breeding ground for "riot, revolution and rape," which they contrasted to the "good, clean, healthy, disciplined, patriotic" teachings of their schools.

The Rev. Roy Thompson, president of Christian Schools of Ohio, called for a legislative investigation of the state's public schools to see if taxpayers are getting their money's worth.

He also urged protesters to continue to organize politically and to vote against foes of church schools.

"We are God-fearing, tax-paying American citizens," he said. "We don't want to fight, but we will."

The loudest cheers of the day greeted his statement that: "We plead to be heard today. Our children belong to us, not to the state of Ohio."

The Rev. Al Janney of Florida, president of American Christian Schools, was at the rally, he said, because "America has its eyes on Ohio. We've drawn the line and we're not going to go any farther. We've never been out in the streets before."

The rally ended soon after a plea for renewed patriotism delivered by a young man standing between two American flags.

Behind him stood a choir, dressed in red, white and blue, humming "America the Beautiful."

Gov. James A. Rhodes at rally.

Heritage Christian School

Rev. Roy Thompson D.D.
Superintentent

Stan Knisley
Administrator

Bruce Witzke

HCS First 11th and 12th Classes

Kevin Folger's
Senior Picture

Honorary Doctorate
from Midwestern

Honorary Doctorate from
Bob Jones Univesity

CLEVELAND BAPTIST WINS 3 'HALOS'

BEST WORSHIP SERVICE — Resurrection Catholic Church, Solon

BEST CHOIR — Mayfield United Methodist Church

BEST CONGREGATIONAL SINGING — Cleveland Baptist Church.

BEST PREACHERS — Rev. Phillip Giessler, St. Thomas Lutheran Church (Rocky River) and Rev. Roy Thompson, Cleveland Baptist Church

FRIENDLIEST CHURCHES — Cleveland Baptist Church, First Assembly of God Church (Lyndhurst), Jehovah's Witnesses (West Park), Madison Ave. Baptist Church, West Park Christian Reformed Church

HOW 'FIRST 50' CHURCHES RATED

| Poor | Fair | Average | Good to Excellent |

KEY TO STAR RATINGS: Churches are rated in four categories: worship service, music, sermon and friendliness. Up to three stars are awarded in each category. Maximum rating therefore is 12 stars.

12 STARS (5)
Community Pentecostal Church of God
Cleveland Baptist Church
St. Augustine's Catholic Church
St. Thomas Lutheran Church (Rocky River)
Plagenz' own service in the park

11 STARS (5)
St. Christopher's-by-the-River
Resurrection Catholic Church
Antioch Baptist Church
Temple Emanu El
First Assembly of God Church (Lyndhurst)

10 STARS (10)
First Church of the Nazarene
Church of the Saviour (Methodist)
Immanuel Lutheran Church
Madison Avenue Baptist Church
Calvary Assembly of God Church
Rocky River United Methodist Church
Cedar Hill Baptist Church
Trinity Cathedral
City Mission
Church of the Covenant

9 STARS (12)
The Chapel
First Community Church (Columbus)
West Shore Unitarian Church
Fairmount Presbyterian Church
Christ the King Lutheran Church
St. Paul Croatian Catholic Church
Epworth Euclid Methodist Church
Parma-South Presbyterian Church
Church of Religious Science
Cove Church (United Methodist)
West Park Christian Reformed Church
Second Mt. Carmel Baptist Church

8 STARS (6)
Bay Presbyterian Church
St. Rose Catholic Church
Lakewood United Methodist Church.
Brith Emeth
First Unitarian Church
Heights Christian Church

7 STARS (6)
First Methodist Church
Euclid Avenue Christian Church
Rocky River Christian Science Church
First Seventh-Day Adventist Church
Jehovah's Witnesses (West Park)
First Congregational Church (No. Ridgeville)

6 STARS (2)
Boulevard United Presbyterian Church
Rocky River United Presbyterian Church

MINI-REVIEWS — No ratings (5)
St. John Episcopal Church
West Blvd. Christian Church
Mayfield United Methodist Church
St. Peter's Episcopal Church
Rockport United Methodist Church

CHAPTER TWELVE

A Forward Reach

*But continue thou in the things which thou hast
learned and hast been assured of, knowing of
whom thou hast learned them.*—II Timothy 3:14

In 1981, nine years after the homegoing of his father figure Dallas Billington, Pastor Thompson said a final goodbye to his mother. Mabel Thompson had suffered from severe dementia. She often didn't recognize family members, including her own children. She lived with Dorothy and Ed for over 30 years, but there were stretches of several months when Roy and Faith would care for her, which deepened their appreciation for Dorothy and Ed. When she went to be with the Lord, it was comforting to know that she was no longer suffering. Despite this loss, Pastor Thompson chose to let the joy of Jesus remain in him as he led the church.

The influence of Cleveland Baptist Church continued to expand in the '80s. When Ronald Reagan was campaigning against President Jimmy Carter for the election of 1980, a rally was held in Cleveland. Pastor Thompson led those in attendance in prayer. Reagan wrote Pastor Thompson a letter stating that he was "touched" by Pastor Thompson's "moving invocation."

Kevin Folger was saved at the age of five when the church was meeting in its first auditorium on Tiedeman. During his teen years, Kevin went through a brief period of inner rebellion. That changed during a missions conference his junior year of high school. Dr. Jack Baskin, who had been a missionary to Korea, was preaching. Through this message, God called Kevin to preach His Word in a full-time capacity. He got serious about his calling and followed the steady example of his father, by developing a servant's heart and a burden for the lost.

Kevin started his preparation for ministry at BBC in 1975. There he met Denise Smith, of Lima, Ohio. Coincidentally, one of the things he had in common with her was that both of their dads were twins. Kevin married Denise a year later when he was 19 years old. Their honeymoon was spent "visiting family," a decision he admittedly regrets. Their son, Kevin, Jr., was born a year later. His young family moved back to Cleveland in May of 1978 after he graduated. Ron Wolvin had left to take a pastorate, which created an opening on the church staff. Kevin Folger was hired. He was thankful for the chance to work alongside not only his pastor, but also his dad.

According to Pastor Thompson, Kevin had some unusual capabilities. He was a self-starter and a self-motivator. He was put in charge of various classes and ministries. He started the Young-at-Heart ministry, which became a highly successful program for the church's 55-and-over crowd. As the years went on, Pastor Thompson felt he had something special. He had watched Kevin grow up. There were few people Pastor Thompson felt were more trustworthy than Bob Folger, and he had observed the manner in which Bob and Nancy raised their children. He knew that character had been instilled in them.

When Kevin Folger joined the staff, it was as a missionary intern. He believed that God was calling him to the foreign mission field. When he took a trip to Singapore in the spring of 1979, the Lord did not give him peace about it. He had a difficult time approaching Pastor Thompson about his future. The church had invested in him, and Pastor Thompson could be intimidating at times. He was worried about the reaction the news that he wasn't going to Singapore would get, but Pastor Thompson wasn't surprised at all. In fact, he said, "I knew you weren't going, but I had to let you figure it out on your own." It was decided that Kevin would remain on staff. His second son, Peter, was born later that year.

In 1982, Dr. Thompson and Kevin Folger were visiting the family of Kyle Scott, who had recently passed away. Comforting those who were experiencing grief was an aspect of the ministry that Dr. Thompson knew was not only important, but a privilege. Years after his retirement, he said that he missed that role more than anything else. On this particular day, however, the future of the church was on his mind. What took place between these two men was something unexpected. For the first time ever, Pastor Thompson mentioned the possibility of Kevin being the next pastor of the church.

Dr. Thompson had found that the best staff members had been people who were raised at the church. Kevin was only 25 years old at the time and had three little boys at home, while Dr. Thompson was not yet 50 years old. Kevin felt honored to be considered but the idea didn't seem realistic. Roy Thompson was a superhero to him. How could he fill those shoes? Over the next couple years, they both prayed for the Lord's leading in their lives and in the life of Cleveland Baptist Church.

Ron Wolvin's son, Dan, joined the staff in 1982, the same year the above exchange transpired. The Wolvins returned to Cleveland Baptist from Tampa, Florida, in September of 1976. They came back so Dan could finish his last two years of high school in Cleveland, which they considered home. He would be enrolled at Heritage during its third academic year. After graduating from Bible college, he was privileged to be part of the church where his father had served. His strong work ethic made him an asset to the church despite having received a prank-loving gene from his father. Four years earlier he had removed Pastor Thompson's toupee during a staff versus alumni basketball game. Dr. Thompson had a history of playing practical jokes himself, and the staff had been taunting the alumni with various threats relative to "secret weapons" that might be pulled out during the game. The story is best told by the culprit himself:

> As Pastor Thomson dribbled down the key to the basket during the first half, I allowed him to pass by undefended and reached up and firmly grasped his toupee. He ran out from under my upstretched hand, which was now in possession of his hairpiece, and I distinctly heard the sound of the tape ripping off his scalp. For approximately three seconds, it seemed all of the air was sucked out of the gym as 600 spectators drew in their breath sharply. Then silence. The gymnasium erupted in laughter and cheering and flash bulbs popped all over the room. The uproar continued all through Pastor's justly awarded two free

throws, for what was clearly a very personal foul. According to Pastor Thompson, the response to people who asked if he ever got me back was, "Sure, I did. I hired him."

While the incident may seem to lack decorum, it is important to remember that Pastor Thompson loved to have a good time, and he was not the type of individual who could dish it out but couldn't take it. He could take a joke, and he was humble enough to appreciate the laugh, even at his own expense. He was also clearly not fond of formalism. It was a moment those in attendance remembered for years to come.

In the summer of 1984, Pastor Thompson mentioned to Dan in passing that he'd be taking his orders from Kevin some day. They had known each other their whole lives. Kevin was just three years older. Kevin graduated from BBC the same year Dan graduated from HCS. It wasn't that he didn't respect Kevin; he did. It wasn't that he didn't think Kevin could do it. It wasn't that he expected to be given that role himself. It was just not something he had ever considered. After 26 years of ministry, it was simply hard for anyone to conceive of someone other than Roy Thompson pastoring Cleveland Baptist Church.

Despite these discussions, nothing was set in stone. For one thing, Kevin was going to have to earn the position. He knew how the church had been built, and he knew how hard-working its people were. Nothing was going to be handed to him. On top of that, ultimately, it would be a matter decided by the people who comprised the church. Pastor Thompson could recommend a candidate, but a proper New Testament church is congregational in polity. Kevin believed that if it was God's will, the Lord would give him favor with the people. His job for the time being was just to do his best for the glory of Jesus Christ.

Bob Folger became principal of HCS while it was meeting in a school building on Bagley Road, the first of its three excursions before returning to the property on Tiedeman in 1992. He hired Larry Frost in 1983. Larry joined Ron Nelson and Dave Cook as anchors of the school for the next 30 years. Bruce Witzke was assistant principal under Bob Folger for two years and became principal in 1984 when the school was meeting on Roadan Road. Bruce would oversee the school for the next 24 years. Al Stone joined the school staff in 1984 and married Ruthy Thompson the following year.

Another valuable addition to the church staff arrived in 1985. Jack Beaver had grown up in a dysfunctional home. His mother had been divorced three times. He had a half-sister that he didn't even know existed until he was a teenager. In 1969, he attended the same church from which, nine years earlier, Vernon Davis and others had come. He thought he was saved, but he was not.

Jack enlisted in the Air Force the following year. He and his girlfriend, Rita, had a decision to make. If they got married, she'd have to go to Germany with him. The other option was to wait four years before marrying. They chose to marry. They were back in the states periodically on leave. Rita's sister invited her to Cleveland Baptist Church, and they began attending sporadically.

In 1976, Jack's time in the Air Force ended and they moved back to Cleveland. Rita began attending services, but Jack wouldn't; so they made a deal. They both had full-time jobs, but Jack wanted more money. Jim and Debbie Flores had offered

Rita an evening job selling soap to friends. It was a program similar to Avon Cosmetics. The deal was that if Rita would sell soap for six months, Jack would come to church for six months.

Jack, still thinking that he was saved, was baptized. In November of 1976, Al Lacy came to town to preach. He delivered a message called "Twelve Inches between Heaven and Hell." The sermon explained the difference between a mental knowledge of the plan of salvation and genuine repentance and faith. As a 27-year-old husband and father, Jack was born again that day. He made changes in his life. He knew he should never drink again, so he decided to sell his booze. He then realized that if he sold his stash, he would be contributing to someone else's drunkenness. He decided to pour his entire collection of liquor down the drain. Unbeknownst to him, the chemicals in the alcohol burned through the plumbing of his sink. His decision, though guided by the Lord, required the employment of a plumber.

The first person Jack led to the Lord was his own grandmother. He wanted to be a soulwinner, but he struggled with self-confidence. He felt the Lord could never really use him for anything. It was when he heard a sermon called "The Barren Fig Tree" that he surrendered to full-time ministry at the age of 30. He stepped out in faith, quit his well-paying job, and enrolled in Hyles-Anderson College. He took his family with him, and after he graduated in 1984, he worked on a church staff in West Virginia for a year. When a pastoral change took place in West Virginia, the Lord called him back to Cleveland.

In 1986 Dan Wolvin, the youth director, had been on staff for four years. He had been groomed by one of the greatest preachers alive. He felt he was ready to pastor. He prepared letters of recommendation and began investigating various places. At the annual missions conference that March, his plans came to a screeching halt. The speaker that was invited was unable to attend, so Dr. Thompson preached instead. One of the messages was on the difference between a burden, a vision, and a call. Dan came forward and surrendered to stay at Cleveland Baptist for as long as God desired him to be there. If he left, it would have to be because God was moving him. Weeks later, revival hit the youth department, and he began to see the Lord blessing his ministry like he had never seen before. He would remain in Cleveland another 15 years.

The church continued to prosper. Bus routes brought in triple-digit numbers of riders. Jack Beaver took over the Young-at-Heart ministry. Bob Folger had a hand in everything. Under the direction of Bruce Witzke, a collection of godly teachers trained children at HCS. Across the many areas of the ministry, lives were conformed to the image of Christ.

Other wise men were being trained to scale cities.

Pastor Thompson and
Kevin Folger

Kevin Folger

Kevin and Denise Folger

Jack Beaver

Dan Wolvin

Dan Wolvin Family

Bus Ministry

RONALD REAGAN

September 17, 1980

Reverend Roy Thompson
Cleveland Baptist Church
4431 Tiedeman Road
Cleveland, Ohio 44144

Dear Reverend Thompson:

It was a pleasure to be with you
at the Rally in Cleveland.

I especially want you to know how
much I appreciated your moving invocation.

My very best wishes to you.

Sincerely,

RONALD REAGAN

901 South Highland Street, Arlington, Virginia 22204

Ronald Reagan's Letter to Pastor Thompson After Rally

CHAPTER THIRTEEN

A Solid Plan

Without counsel purposes are disappointed...—
Proverbs 15:22

Humility was the key to unlocking God's will for Cleveland Baptist Church. Pastor Thompson always viewed the church as belonging not to himself, but to Jesus Christ. He said, "If I am God's man, then I ought to have the desire to make sure somebody is going to be here to carry on." Pastor Thompson observed that there were very few sound, Bible-believing churches that lasted 100 years. Most of them died when the founding pastor died or left. Most of them lacked preparation for the future.

In both the Old and New Testament, God always had someone to take over. Moses turned his leadership role over to Joshua even when his strength wasn't abated and his eyes weren't dim. Paul turned churches over to other pastors. Dr. Thompson said, "A younger, more youthful person with knowledge of the times and the future needed to step in. It was a very simple plan; it wasn't really profound."

Cleveland Baptist was expanding. There was growth in finances, missions, and other ministries. Pastor Thompson refused to allow God's work in Cleveland to cease. Just as corporations plan for the future, this church would plan for the future. There could be no success without a successor. In his sermons, he slowly prepared the people for his eventual departure from the pastorate.

While the staff was aware of the future plans, the church was getting used to Kevin Folger's preaching. When Pastor Thompson was out traveling, Kevin assumed leadership responsibilities. Dr. Thompson liked to have a strong associate pastor because he was usually out at least one or two Sundays every month.

In a 1989 meeting, Dr. Thompson asked the deacons to vote on whether or not Kevin Folger should become co-pastor. They unanimously approved. Kevin was grateful for the role into which God was placing him, but he wanted to know how the church felt about it. He proposed that the church vote as well, and Dr. Thompson agreed.

In 1990, Pastor Thompson told the church that if it approved the plan, Kevin Folger would officially become co-pastor. The vote would be taken on Sunday night, June 6th. Kevin felt it was best for him not to be there the night the vote took place. Instead, the Folger family would depart for a two-week vacation out west.

Kevin, Denise, and their boys left for Yellowstone National Park the Wednesday before the vote. The results were delivered to them via telephone four days later. All five of them were huddled around a pay phone when they learned that 98 percent of Cleveland Baptist Church had approved Kevin Folger becoming the co-pastor. There were only six votes cast by individuals who did not support the plan. Pastor Thompson said, "It was not just my desire. The church had to accept it, and it wholeheartedly did."

The vote itself was a mere formality. While he hadn't technically been co-pastor prior to the vote, it seemed as though Kevin had been serving in that role already to most of the members of the church. The vote wasn't controversial because nothing major seemed to be changing. The decision did bring implications along with it. Pastor Folger would have an increasing amount of involvement in decisions concerning the staff, inviting preachers, church associations, financial matters, and other areas. He would also become the pastor upon the death or resignation of Pastor Thompson, though nobody, including Kevin, knew how long that would be.

It was clear that having an immediate plan of succession would be better for the church than having to scramble to get candidates in or to have an interim pastor in the event of the unexpected. Dr. Thompson said he would probably resign by the time he was 65, but in June of 1990, he was only 57. They began preaching alternately in services, and people became more and more comfortable and familiar with the future pastor.

In many instances, the people of a church have a deep loyalty to their founding pastor. Cleveland Baptist Church had grown up with Roy Thompson. He had thundered from the pulpit, comforted in trials, shepherded his flock, and encouraged believers for 32 years. It stands to reason that accepting another man in his place would be difficult. The people knew Kevin Folger's family. They knew the kind of home in which he was raised. They knew the convictions and principles of his father. They observed his character. They also understood that rejecting this plan would be tantamount to believing that Dr. Thompson didn't understand God's will for the future of the church. They got on board and a smooth segue between pastors was now ensured. The future of the church was bright.

The wise man didn't keep his methods for scaling to himself; he trained another wise man.

CLEVELAND BAPTIST CHURCH
4431 Tiedeman Rd.
Cleveland, Ohio 44144   (216) 671-2822
1989 DIRECTORY

Rev. Roy Thompson
Pastor - Founder

Rev. Kevin Folger
Co-Pastor

CHAPTER FOURTEEN

A Permanent Home

...shewing to the generation to come the praises of the Lord, and his strength, and his wonderful works that he hath done.—Psalm 78:4

In the early days of Heritage Christian School, there was no school building and no lease at buildings on Bagley, Holland, or Roadan Road. The school used the church's facilities. Twice a week, the entire building had to be switched from a school to a church. The sacrifice involved was significant. Dr. Thompson's role in the battle that was fought over Christian education was appreciated. It wasn't all about methodology, curriculum, and facilities. It was a privilege just to have a Christian school, no matter where it met or how many times it had to move, and no matter how great of a command the teachers had of calculus or governmental theory.

The relationship between the school and the church had always been important. Since its inception in 1974, the school had been a major part of Cleveland Baptist Church. On one hand the church had 17 years of fruitful ministry before the school ever existed, and the church had many other ministries in addition to the school. On the other hand, the school had been the largest ministry of the church in terms of finances, staffing, and other resources. While some children were educated at home and some attended public schools, a significant chunk of CBC's core families chose to have their children receive their education at HCS. The church and the school had inseparable ties.

In 1990, the school building where HCS was meeting was a Brooklyn city school on Roadan Road. Brooklyn's Department of Education, however, informed Bruce Witzke that HCS's lease would not be renewed. The way the Brooklyn school system was constituted was such that its high school was too close to its younger grades. It was not a good situation because of the negative influence the older students had on the younger students. The district would need the building that HCS was using in order to maintain separation between the two groups of children. HCS was confronted with yet another move. Some of the staff members had been a part of three moves already. Pastor Thompson, Pastor Folger, and Bruce Witzke sensed that it was time to construct a permanent building for the school. Others agreed. The cost was $1.7 million.

Plans for the new building were in the works. As the design phase progressed, the school returned to the church building for the 1991-1992 and 1992-1993 school years. School was not easy to operate under these conditions. Some classes met in the basement. Green pews that were more than 20 years old were used on the second floor. Students had to grab a desktop in the morning and bring it with them throughout the day. The principal's office was in a house that the church owned. Six modular classrooms were placed behind the church building for additional space.

To minimize costs, much of the work on the new building was done by staff and church members as opposed to professional crews. Fortunately, CBC had members with skill and expertise in construction. Roger Hoffman was the general contractor. He had grown up in Cleveland, off Bellaire Road. One night in 1961, he and two of his friends were driving around Cleveland and Lakewood looking for individuals they might like to meet, preferably females. They saw three pretty young ladies unloading suitcases on W. 117th Street. They stopped the car and asked if they could help. Joyce Holbert, her older sister, and her friend Kathy were returning from a weekend trip. They were from Pennsylvania and had gone back home to visit. A little help with their luggage was appreciated.

Joyce observed that Roger was outgoing and friendly in addition to gentlemanly in his offer to help them. A recent graduate of West Tech High School, he was raised Presbyterian and was not saved. Joyce, having grown up in a Baptist church, had heard the gospel clearly and was saved already. Their relationship progressed, and they were married in Pennsylvania two years later.

In 1965, two years after he was married, Roger's mother, Julia, was working in the advertising department at *The Plain Dealer.* Faith Thompson made a phone call to place an ad for Cleveland Baptist Church in the religion section of the paper, and Julia answered. She told Faith that she would like to visit the church. Her daughter-in-law was Baptist, and it sounded like an interesting church. She visited alone on a Sunday morning, and she got saved. She was excited, and she told Joyce that she had previously never heard of salvation as a free gift. Joyce and Roger began attending and after a couple weeks, Roger heard a message from Jeremiah 8:20: "The harvest is past, the summer is ended, and we are not saved." At age 22, Roger responded to the gospel invitation and was saved.

Roger was scripturally baptized after his salvation, and he and Joyce were quickly assimilated into the church family. Roger was a steelworker but found time to help with various odd jobs around the church building. He and Roy Thompson quickly developed a friendship. They had similar personalities. Roger fit right in with Roy, Larry, Ron, and Bob. They had a good time taking verbal jabs at one another. In reference to their large noses, Roy and Roger called each other the "the hook and the beak." In September of 1975, drafting and woodshop classes were being added to the HCS curriculum for its second year of school. Roger Hoffman was given the opportunity to teach. He quit his job at U.S. Steel and joined the school staff. The students affectionately nicknamed Roger "The Professor."

As time went on, Roger joined a group called Builders for Christ that Pastor Thompson assembled in the 1980s. The men traveled to Africa, Haiti, Brazil, Canada, and Mexico constructing church buildings, Bible colleges, schools, and other facilities for gospel-preaching churches. Through this experience, the Lord prepared Roger to oversee the completion of a 40,000 square foot structure that would house a school that taught God's Word.

Roger Hoffman later recalled that in the few instances where work was outsourced to "professionals," it was inferior to the work performed by those who were spiritually invested in the project. Dan Wolvin, Bruce Witzke, Dave Cook, and others operated machinery, poured cement, and put up rafters in addition to a myriad of other jobs. The construction was going smoothly, but a hindrance would arise.

CBC member Joel Spafford had been a trustee at his previous church, which closed. It had $100,000 in its bank account and its constitution said that in this event, the funds must be given to a like-minded church. Because of this man's role in both churches, Cleveland Baptist got the money. Pastor Thompson stepped out in faith and broke ground on HCS's $1.7 million school building with just the first $100,000. That initial capital disappeared quickly. Unfortunately, no banks were willing to give loans. Banks tend to hesitate giving loans when the project for which the capital is being solicited is already underway. It appeared that the project was going to be stuck.

God delights to intervene at times that seem impossible because in those times it is most evident that the glory belongs to Him. Right around the time the school building project was running out of funding, Bruce Witzke's son, Matt, was seriously ill and required professional medical attention. It was a time of trial for the Witzke family. Bruce had been spending a lot of time at the hospital due to the circumstances. He made many acquaintances. One of them was a fellow believer named Frank Giganti, who was a member of the church that became Broadview Heights Baptist Church. Bruce mentioned the status of the project and that the church could not secure a loan. Frank happened to have a brother-in-law who was a loan officer for a bank in Akron that specialized in giving loans to churches. He connected Bruce and Pastor Thompson with his brother-in-law, and within a week, the paperwork was signed on a loan for the remaining capital.

In the spring of 1993, the school building was about six months away from its debut. Much of the work had been finished, but some final touches were still needed before its opening. Including gymnasium locker rooms, the school needed close to 500 lockers. It had none. Bob Folger was the church's business manager at the time. He requested an estimate from a provider and was told the lockers would cost $52,000. He was not thrilled about the hefty price tag, but it was necessary. He mentioned to Bruce Witzke that he was going to have to bite the bullet and spend the money.

While praying about and pondering how to proceed, Bruce ran into an old friend named Rick Pflaum. Rick's father, Al, had been in the janitorial supply business since the '50s. Al had made a sales call on Cleveland Baptist Church when it was meeting in the house on Memphis Avenue. He established a relationship with Bob Folger, and his company became the church's vendor for supplies. Even when Al's son, Rick, took over the family business, CBC continued as a client. By 1993, that hadn't changed.

One day Rick Pflaum was at Lorain County Community College to make a sales call. He was told that the individual for whom he was looking was not available because he was in a warehouse. He was told he could look for him if he wanted. The college had undergone some remodeling and the warehouse was filled with leftover odds and ends. When Rick walked through it, he noticed hundreds of lockers that were not in use. He asked about them and was told the college was hoping to get rid of them. The next time Bruce crossed paths with Rick, he asked him if he knew of anywhere to get lockers for a good price. It was a shot in the dark. He had no idea what Rick had seen on his last visit to the college. Rick, floored by how unlikely the coincidence was, put Bruce and Bob in touch with the right people at LCCC.

Bob and Bruce met with a representative from the college and explained that they needed about 500 lockers. At first the representative did not know Bruce and Bob were from a school. Many foundries, factories, and other professional environments used lockers too. When they explained that they were there on behalf of HCS and asked what the cost would be, they were astounded at the answer. There wouldn't be a cost. The lockers would be donated because HCS was a non-profit organization. Not only would they be free, but they were also in nearly perfect condition, as college students aren't as rough on them as high school students are. God was generously and graciously providing for a church that sought to teach another generation to honor His Word. As a result, the church saved more than $50,000.

The new building was ready for the 1993-1994 school year. It included a gymnasium, a library, a cafeteria with a kitchen, 19 classrooms, and computer and science labs. The church was excited. After 18 years of school taking place in a nomadic way, there was now a first-class, professional facility for the purpose of training young people to live according to God's Word.

It was a testimony to what God could do if His people truly believed in the importance of developing future wise men.

HCS Construction

Heritage Christian School Gym

Heritage Christian School
Home of the Patriots

Heritage Christian School
A ministry of the Cleveland Baptist Church
4403 Tiedeman Road
Brooklyn, Ohio 44144

CHAPTER FIFTEEN

A Smooth Transition

And the Lord said,...as I was with Moses, so I will be with thee.—Joshua 3:7

D ue to sin, all bodies deteriorate. Health fails. People slow down. This is true in all professions. In the ministry, many pastors reach a peak in their careers. Their age at this peak varies depending on the individual. A young man has strength and energy but lacks experience and wisdom. An older man has experience and wisdom but lacks strength and energy. The peak is the point at which these two opposing timeframes meet. A pastor peaks when one side of the spectrum does not seem to come at the expense of the other. It is possible to be productive and effective after the peak has passed, but it takes more effort to combat the natural decline.

Dr. Thompson felt that many pastors reach their peak and then coast. Many do not put forth the effort needed to resist the stagnation that comes with slowing down. Dr. Thompson did not resign because he was afraid that he would coast. In fact, he even said that some of the highlights of his ministry took place after he stepped down from the pastorate. He did, however, believe that the surest way to avoid the very *appearance* of coasting would be to have a man in his prime as the pastor of Cleveland Baptist Church. He didn't want the church to slow down nor give the slightest impression that it was slowing down. He said, "Jesus must increase and we must decrease. As we get older, we often don't want to decrease. We want to keep going and keep climbing, but it gets too steep for us. It is best to find someone who shares the same vision, doctrine, principles, and desires and just get out of the way."

Pastor Thompson also took notice of what happened in many other churches when the founding pastor neared the end of his career. He observed that in many cases, a pastor who had devoted his life to building a church had a very difficult time "keeping his hands off it" once it was under the direction of another man. The result was usually strife. Divisions would take place as allegiances were questioned. Members would leave. He also observed that under a younger man, doctrine would often change. Standards would be lowered and compromises would be made. Modern philosophies would replace the time-tested, proven, God-honoring approach to ministry. After much prayer, he discerned that God was leading him to resign.

Dr. Thompson had prepared Kevin Folger to the best of his ability and firmly believed that proper doctrine, standards, and separation would continue. The church loved Dr. Thompson, but also understood that "[their] faith should not stand in the wisdom of men, but in the power of God" (I Corinthians 2:5). Some congregations are so loyal to a man that once he is gone, they stop serving God. Their eyes were on the man, not on God, but Cleveland Baptist Church understood the importance of "looking unto Jesus" (Hebrews 12:2).

At the age of 62, the Lord had used Roy Thompson to accomplish more than he ever imagined. He calculated that in his 37 years as pastor he preached 8,000 sermons at Cleveland Baptist Church. He baptized about 4,000 people. He married nearly 600 couples. He conducted about 800 funerals. The church grew from one room full of people to 2,000 on Sunday mornings, and on some occasions 2,500 or more. Most importantly, an inestimable number of souls came to Jesus Christ for salvation under his ministry.

The church became aware of Pastor Thompson's decision to resign in early 1995. The first eight months of that year was a busy time. Pastor Thompson organized a trip to the Holy Land. He was scheduled to preach in a number of meetings. Pastor Folger was tasked with organizing Dr. Thompson's final services as pastor. It was decided that his last sermon as pastor would be preached on September 3rd, 1995. Six weeks later he would depart for the Philippines. Dr. Thompson wanted the people to have no choice but to go to Pastor Folger with their difficulties. He knew that if he were accessible, some people would still view him as their pastor. He also had a deep burden for and connection with the people of the Philippines, his home away from home. He had been looking forward to spending more time there, as well as more time in Haiti and Brazil.

Pastor Folger had been co-pastor for five years and on staff for 18 years. He had held his Doctor of Divinity degree for three years. Two of his children were in high school and one had graduated. He had spent his entire life at Cleveland Baptist Church. It was certainly a distinct honor, but a heavy responsibility was falling on his shoulders. He hadn't yet realized the weight of it.

He went home that night and didn't sleep well. In the past, no matter how big a problem was, he could always send it to another office because there was someone responsible there. Now he would be the one accountable to the Lord Jesus Christ for this church. He wondered about the people and how they would respond to him, despite having voted for him. He wondered about the finances. As to what was going through his mind at the time, he recalled, "For a man who had never been a pastor before to step into that role, considering the size of a church like Cleveland Baptist, and to follow a man with the stature of Dr. Roy Thompson, I didn't know how big that moment was."

Wise men are not easy to replace.

Pastor Thompson and Pastor Folger

Pastor and Mrs. Thompson

Pastor Thompson's Last Service as the Pastor

CHAPTER SIXTEEN
A New Era

For this cause left I thee in Crete, that thou
shouldest set in order the things that are
wanting...—Titus 1:5

The position Pastor Kevin Folger was stepping into was filled with challenges, but God had the right man for the right age. For years, Dr. Thompson publicly told Pastor Folger, "You're going to have to deal with things that I've never had to deal with." With a new era beginning and new obstacles on the horizon, he streamlined the church's day-to-day functions by updating its technology with computer-oriented systems. He also assembled his staff to best equip the church. He asked Dan Wolvin to be his senior associate pastor in addition to making other personnel changes.

Luke and Pam Brown returned to Cleveland from Pennsylvania to join the HCS faculty in 1995 but later joined the church staff. They both grew up at Cleveland Baptist Church. Luke first attended in 1974 as a nine-year-old boy. His parents had been searching for a church home, and when they heard

Dr. Thompson open and preach from the Word of God, they were hooked. Luke's father, Ira Brown, a long-time carpenter, groundskeeper, and construction worker, joined the church maintenance staff in 1978. The Lord took him home in 2001, but he was a prayer warrior and a faithful man of God for more than 50 years.

In 1978, the same year Pastor Folger was hired, Luke was 13 years old. He had heard and was aware of the gospel but had not received Christ. As he was on Cypress Avenue in Old Brooklyn working his paper route one day, the Holy Spirit said to his heart, "If you died today, you'd go to hell. Why don't you get saved?" At that moment, Luke asked Jesus Christ to save his soul.

Seven years later, Luke was called to full-time ministry under the preaching of deaf evangelist Reggie Rempel. The Lord confronted Luke's heart as he thought, "If God can use him, then God can use me." In the summer of 1988, he married Pam Thompson, who had received eternal life as a little girl at Cleveland Baptist Church. They prepared themselves for ministry at Fairhaven Baptist College and served at a Baptist church in Pennsylvania before returning to their home church to serve under its new pastor.

One of Pastor Folger's first goals was to expand the property to the south. Parking was becoming a major problem. At the time, the southern border of the church's property line was the bus garage. American Greetings allowed the church to use its parking lot as well as American Road. As gracious as that was, problems persisted because it wasn't just a few cars that needed to be parked there. It was more than 200. A solution was still needed because visitors would sometimes pull into the parking lot, find no spaces, and leave because they didn't have anywhere to park. Complicating matters was the fact that the owner of the property had spurned the church's offers to purchase it. In the '70s and '80s, offers were turned down because the owner's perceived value of the property was vastly overestimated. The church was landlocked.

A successful pastor is one who not only has a vision for the future, but is also able to transfer his vision to the people he leads. The quandary with the parking lot led to a pastor with a vision; a pastor with a vision led to a church with a vision. Pastor Folger asked the church to pray earnestly and fervently. Some of Cleveland Baptist's men walked the perimeter of the property, claiming Joshua 1:3, "Every place that the sole of your foot shall tread upon, that have I given unto you." Due to these circumstances the initiative was named "The Promised Land." In 1999, God met the need and a deal was brokered. The price tag was high, but the property was expanded. The area that was purchased was paved and now allows ample parking space as well as room to keep buses. Perhaps most importantly, the fruition of the vision was proof to the church that God, indeed, had led in the transition to Pastor Folger.

The ministry was still growing, both physically and spiritually. In 1997 and 1998, bus attendance averaged over 600 and hit 1,000 on a few occasions. The Saturday morning bus workers' meeting consistently drew between 70 and 80 people. The church's membership reached its all-time peak.

Due to its rich history and rare size for an independent Baptist church, CBC enjoyed a degree of national influence. While proper independent Baptist churches reflect the New Testament principles of being self-funded and autonomous, fellowship is still a factor. No other church has authority over another. They are not part of a convention. They are not subject to the mandates from a headquarters. However, pastors do need to meet to refresh one another. Churches cooperate with camps, youth programs, and help one another with church plants. Fellowships are formed in which pastors influence one another. CBC had been part of the Baptist Bible Fellowship for most of its history. This was the same fellowship in which Dr. Thompson had gone against the grain with his disapproval of Bob Harrington's ministry (see chapter 11).

Dr. Thompson was becoming skeptical of the direction in which the BBF was going by the 1980s. It had been in existence since 1950. It owned BBC, the institution from which many of Cleveland Baptist's most public servants had graduated. Not long after Pastor Folger graduated, the college began to shift because the churches that comprised the fellowship began to shift. Their music became more contemporary. Their positions on the correct Bible version weakened. Their lines of separation from the world became less clear.

The most significant move in that direction was its accreditation. Pastor Folger felt strongly that there was no reason for BBC to get accredited. It trains pastors and missionaries. It does not exist for secular work. When a college is accredited, it must submit to regulations put forth by institutions with agendas that are diametrically opposed to the agenda of a New Testament church. This could be acceptable for colleges training young people to work in the business world, but it is not acceptable for a college that exists to train preachers of God's Word. When Kevin Folger became co-pastor of Cleveland Baptist Church, he began attending BBF meetings and began noticing its left-ward shift.

Sam Davison was pastor of Southwest Baptist Church in Oklahoma City, Oklahoma when the paradigm of BBF was changing. When Pastor Folger heard him preach, it was clear to him that Sam Davison would take a firm stance on the fundamentals of the faith, separation, and music. He would oppose the evangelical mentality. When he was elected president of BBF in 1994, Pastor Folger thought, "If anyone can bring this fellowship back to where it should be, it is this man." Four years passed under his presidency and the time came for another election. One candidate sided with Sam Davison and Pastor Folger while the other held the opposite views. When the fellowship elected the candidate that Pastor Folger did not favor, he realized that if Sam Davison couldn't restore the BBF to what it used to be, then nobody could. He decided he was finished with it.

The rift deepened in 1998 when Sam Davison brought Pacific Coast Baptist College from San Dimas, California to Oklahoma City. It had previously been associated with the BBF. Even though Oklahoma City and Springfield are nearly 300 miles apart, the left-leaning pastors in the BBF did not want the right-leaning pastors to run a college so close to BBC. The two parties represented totally different philosophies of ministry. Compromise was not an option. Heartland withdrew its association with the BBF. An organization called "Friends of Heartland" was then formed. This was an opportunity for the pastors who supported Heartland to encourage one another in their commitment to God-honoring methods of ministry.

Cleveland Baptist Church hosted a Friends of Heartland meeting two years later. The idea of starting a new fellowship was proposed and garnered considerable support. Pastor Bruce

Turner of Tampa, Florida, took the lead in promoting it. The idea was approved and the Global Independent Baptist Fellowship was launched. Pastor Folger was at first reluctant about it because of what he had seen transpire in the BBF. After a year he began to see the value in it. He felt it was important because the way pastors are influenced at fellowship meetings affects the churches they lead. Each local body of Christ is either edified or damaged by what shapes its pastor's positions.

Pastor Folger was elected moderator of the GIBF in 2004 and was instrumental in organizing it. He met with its other leaders and spent several days clearly defining its doctrinal positions and laying out its constitution and bylaws. This endeavor brought firmness and the possibility for longevity to this new fellowship. Pastor Folger's role ensured that it would officially and publicly stand for that which the BBF had decades ago stood. He remained moderator until 2008, and CBC hosted one of its 2010 meetings.

Since becoming senior pastor in 1995, Kevin Folger has enjoyed the privilege of having a national platform. He has preached not only in GIBF meetings, but in the Sword of the Lord conferences in North Carolina as well as the Spiritual Leadership conferences in California. He attributes these opportunities to his association with Cleveland Baptist Church, not to himself. He said, "Dr. Thompson bridged so many different areas and so many people knew of him. I don't preach in those meetings because of who I am, but because of who this church is." The creation and development of the GIBF showed that Cleveland Baptist's commitment to doctrinal purity and godly living had not changed.

Promised Land

Ira and Shirley Brown

Luke and Pam Brown

Sam Davison

CHAPTER SEVENTEEN
A Real People

*For we know that if our earthly house of this
tabernacle were dissolved, we have a building of
God, an house not made with hands, eternal in the
heavens. —II Corinthians 5:1*

I t would be inaccurate to portray the history of any church as consisting of nothing but good things. There would be no such thing as good without the possibility of bad. There can be no such thing as health without the possibility of sickness, and no courage without the possibility of danger. Born-again believers are forgiven of their sin; they are saved eternally, but until they die physically, their sin nature remains. A consequence of man's sin nature is that evil pervades the world. While this may be contrary to the teachings of a number of mainline denominations, it is clearly found in Scripture. There is no utopia in a sin-cursed world.

Many converts wrongly assume that all of their troubles will disappear when they get saved, a promise that is not found in Scripture. Atheists and critics label this fact as the "problem of evil." They say that because of the presence of evil and suffering,

God cannot be both all-loving and all-powerful. They contend that if He is all-loving, and *wants* to destroy evil but *cannot*, then He is not all-powerful. They further argue that if He is all-powerful, and *can* destroy evil, but *will not*, then He is not all-loving. They are wrong. He is so powerful that He has created an eternal place that has neither evil nor suffering. He loves so deeply that He offers every person free entrance to this perfect eternity where there is no suffering. What He won't do is force it on them. He allows them to choose. He also commands people not to sin, but they sin anyway, and their sin brings consequences. He is not the source of the problem; people are. Those who have received His salvation are on their way to an eternity free of imperfection, but before they get there, they must cling to Him through the suffering of this present world.

When hardships come, many believers turn away from God. They mistakenly ask, "How could a loving God do this? If He really loved me, He wouldn't do this." This logic, however, asserts that the character of God depends on the circumstances of the individual. God's character never changes, no matter how easy or difficult an individual's life becomes. According to God's Word, difficulties either chasten a believer for sin or lead him to seek God's comfort through the trial.

All people must choose whether trials will lead them to God for comfort or push them away from God in resentment. Cleveland Baptist Church has gone through hard times. Its people have walked through valleys of tragedy. They are real people. They live in an imperfect, sin-filled world. They deal with trials. They are confronted with sorrow and grief. They feel pain. The most difficult trials that bring the heaviest sorrow and the deepest pain tend to be the ones that are least expected. Just as this is true today, it has been true historically.

In many cases, much can be gleaned from the way certain individuals and families respond to God in the midst of unexpected crises. Also helpful to consider are the examples of those who help them through their hardships. The people of Cleveland Baptist Church have banded together to rally around those who have found themselves in their darkest hour of sorrow. It would be impossible to describe every major adversity that a church the size of Cleveland Baptist has faced in 55 years, and some incidents have affected the church as a whole more than others. For the sake of space and time, the stories of two individuals will be told.

Garry and Lois Douglas began attending Cleveland Baptist Church in 1992. They enrolled their children in Heritage Christian School. They had two daughters, Jennifer and Cyndi, and a son, Garry Jr.

Upon graduating from high school, Jennifer went to Crown College in Powell, Tennessee. While Jennifer was in college, her younger sister, Cyndi, worked a bus route as a teenager. She loved the bus ministry. She wanted to be a Christian school teacher. She wanted to impact young lives with the life-changing teachings of Jesus Christ and with the salvation that is found in Him. She prayed and believed that this was God's will for her life. She graduated from HCS in 1999. Crown College was a wise choice. It offered a course of study that would equip her for her path in ministry. Having an older sister there to make for a smooth adjustment to college life was another plus, so she left for Tennessee in August.

On September 25th, Cyndi was 18 years old and only a month into her new life as a college student when she was invited to attend a birthday party. She had been out on visitation the afternoon before the party, inviting people to attend church services the next day. Later that evening, she and four friends, all female students at Crown, were backing out of a driveway on their way to the party. Their destination was not far; it was on the same road as the college.

Shannon Ratliff should have been at work that night; instead, the 20-year-old was drinking. His blood alcohol was .23 percent. Drinking and driving was nothing new to him; he had already been arrested for it twice. He chose to violate his restricted license and drove his Ford Mustang onto Beaver Creek Drive, the same road onto which the girls were turning. He collided with their Buick at approximately 90 miles per hour. Both Cyndi and the driver died instantly. Two of the other three passengers suffered broken pelvises.

Pastor Folger was contacted by the college's authorities as soon as they were made aware of the incident. He faced one of his most difficult moments as a pastor. He had to call the Douglas family to tell them that their youngest daughter, who had just received assurance of her salvation a week earlier, was with her Savior. Cyndi's brother, 15 at the time, answered the phone. He saw Pastor Folger's name on the caller ID. It was after 11:00 p.m. on Saturday night. He wondered if the call had something to do with pack-a-pew Sunday the next morning. Pastor asked to speak with his father. As his dad received the news, the expression on his face revealed the devastation he felt. Jennifer Douglas was not far from the scene when she learned of the tragedy. Pastor Folger's son, Peter, was also a student at

Crown at the time and was there to help Jennifer in any way that he could. Only the presence of the God of all comfort could provide what the Douglas family needed.

The next day the church heard what had taken place. They would never speak with their fellow laborer again. They would never see her become a teacher. She would not return to the bus ministry during summer break. The people of Cleveland Baptist Church lifted the Douglas family up in prayer. The grief experienced by her immediate family as well as her church family was overwhelming.

Shannon Ratliff was charged with two counts of aggravated vehicular homicide and three counts of vehicular assault. Two years later he was convicted and given a prison sentence with a maximum of 26 years. While it was good to know that he would not be endangering other lives on the road, his sentence wouldn't bring Cyndi back. The consequences for sin are not limited to the sinner alone. They affect others.

The Douglas family didn't turn their backs on God. Naturally, they had questions as to why it happened, but they allowed God to draw them to Himself for grace to get through it instead of accusing Him of lacking love for them. They take comfort in knowing they will see her again. Three of the people Cyndi had invited to church just hours before she died attended the services the following morning and got saved. The Douglas family is proud of this legacy that their daughter left. Her father said, "You can't get over it. You just get through it."

Cyndi's sister, Jennifer, and her husband, Matthew, are in full-time ministry. Her brother, Garry, and his wife, Tina, have worked a bus route for several years. The incident was a reminder of the importance of salvation in light of the unpredictability of life.

This tragedy taught Cyndi's family and church to be thankful for her 18 years of life instead of being angry about the years they didn't get to see. It was a testament to how precious life is. It was a reminder that God's people must fully appreciate life because they do not know when it will end.

Romans 12:15 says to "weep with them that weep" and Galatians 6:2 says, "Bear ye one another's burdens, and so fulfill the law of Christ." John and Cheryl Williamson were among those who prayed for the Douglas family. John, 41 at the time, had grown up with a single mother on the west side of Cleveland. They were Catholic. When John graduated from high school in 1976, he started working various factory jobs. A co-worker of his at Foseco in Berea named Marty Coulter invited him to Cleveland Baptist Church. He had never been there and took his co-worker up on the offer. He got saved in April of 1983 at the age of 24. He was baptized and started out in ministry right away. Within six months, he was driving a bus that picked up children for church.

Although they had never met, the same Sunday that John was saved, Cheryl Younger was baptized. Cheryl was also relatively new to the church. Months prior, she had been searching the ads in the *Sun Post* for a babysitter for her son, Vince. Never having heard of Cleveland Baptist, she noticed an ad for babysitting services placed by Dee Drake. When they spoke on the phone, Cheryl learned that all of Dee's spots were taken, but Dee referred her to a friend named Janet Mickey. Janet Mickey became a regular babysitter for Vince. Cheryl was impressed by how kindly Janet treated her and her son. Janet and her husband, Bob, invited Cheryl to church countless times, but she was reluctant. She had received tracts on her door from

CBC for the past four years but was still not interested until Janet decided to sweeten the deal. Janet offered a week of free babysitting if Cheryl would go to church; Cheryl agreed.

Cheryl didn't get saved right away, but the compassion of the people stood out to her. They took an interest in her. She kept coming back. Bob and Janet had been praying that she would get saved. One Sunday night after church, they went over to her house to approach her about her soul. She got saved that night. She was baptized and started attending the college and career class under the leadership of Roger Hoffman. It was there that she crossed paths with John Williamson. After spending time with one another, they realized that the Lord was bringing their lives together, and they were married in January of 1985.

John left factory work and entered the healthcare profession not long after his wedding. He became a technician in the cardiac ICU at University Hospitals. His co-workers and patients found him helpful, genuine, and caring. Months after they were married, Cheryl was expecting a son. Clint was born in 1986. The Williamsons enrolled both Vince and Clint in Heritage Christian School. Over the years, both of them took advantage of opportunities to serve through a variety of ministries. Cleveland Baptist Church was the center of this family's life. Vince graduated from HCS and eventually moved to Pennsylvania.

In 2001, three years before Clint's graduation, John sensed the Lord prompting him to enroll in HBI. He wanted to improve his knowledge of God's Word. After being actively involved in church for 17 years, he had developed a spiritual hunger for the precious words of the Lord. He took at least one class every semester. His favorite verse was Psalm 46:10, "Be still and know that I am God."

Five years after enrolling in HBI, John's desire to help others resulted in his willingness to install a gutter for a widow on Saturday, May 6th, 2006. The widow was the mother of one of his co-workers. The job required the use of a ladder. He and Clint planned to borrow one after eating lunch with Cheryl. When they picked up the ladder, John decided to sit in the back of the pick-up truck while Clint drove.

As John and Clint headed down the ramp exiting I-71, the ladder began to shift. John reached for it but lost his balance. He fell over the side of the truck and hit his head on the ground. Clint saw it in the rearview mirror, got out, and called 9-1-1. He was a nursing student at the time and understood the severity of what had taken place. He did the best he could to hold his father up. He called his mom. She got to the scene just before the ambulance arrived. They followed the ambulance to the hospital. John had a broken shoulder, broken ribs, and significant inflammation of his brain. He would undergo an emergency procedure to remove part of his skull which proved to be unsuccessful. He was put in an induced coma. Nine days later, at the age of 47, John Williamson slipped into eternity. He was in the presence of the Lamb of God, who loved him and died for him.

John was so well-liked at church and at work that his funeral was attended by 985 people. This was the highest turnout the funeral home had ever seen. John's death affected the entire church. All of their friends were members. They were part of the bus ministry, HCS, and Sunday school. He was someone almost everyone either knew or knew of, and suddenly he was gone.

John worked with doctors from all over the world, many of whom heard the gospel of Jesus Christ for the first time at his memorial service. The people of Cleveland Baptist reached out to the Williamson family. They brought meals, but more importantly, they gave their time to provide comfort and company. Jim and Joyce Jones took over their bus route for a month. John's co-workers at the hospital hung a picture of him outside the cardiac ICU, along with a Scripture verse: Psalm 46:10.

The way Cheryl handled this time of overwhelming adversity was an example to the rest of the church. She displayed Christ-likeness amidst suffering. She used the opportunity to talk with bus riders about the reality of death. She said, "At first I was very sad because it was not what I had planned for my life; but our lives are not our own, and that became very apparent to me. This was God's plan. I may not understand it, but He knows what is best for me. He is drawing me closer to Him, and that is what is best for me. Going to Him in prayer brings tremendous comfort." She continued to work her bus route and serve. She continued to read the Bible and spend time alone with God.

While Cleveland Baptist is a great church, it is also a realistic one. Building a foundation upon the rock of Jesus Christ does not make one exempt from storms. Rather, it provides a source of strength from which to survive the storm. The people of Cleveland Baptist Church are susceptible to trials and tribulations just like all others in this world are. Even in the valleys, it is a church that is committed to honoring Christ. He is worthy of praise and faithfulness even when His people suffer.

No man is exempt from suffering simply because he is wise.

Cyndi Douglas

John and Cheryl Williamson and
Cheryl's Mom

CHAPTER EIGHTEEN

A Debt Paid

...the borrower is servant to the lender. —Proverbs 22:7

I n the first five years of the 21st century, the staff of the church underwent changes. After 19 fruitful years of full-time service to the Lord, Dan Wolvin responded to God's call and became pastor of North Columbus Baptist Church. The church was planted out of Cleveland Baptist in 1991. Matt Ewing had grown up at CBC, spent some time away from the Lord, but got married and re-dedicated his life. He and his wife and others traveled between Cleveland and Columbus every Saturday and Sunday to visit and hold services. Pastor Folger, then co-pastor of CBC, preached North Columbus Baptist's organizational service. There were 36 charter members.

Within a few years, a church building was secured and the congregation no longer had to use a school for its meetings. Attendance reached 250 on big days and averaged about 175. In Cleveland, Pastor Folger was thrilled with the job Dan

Wolvin was doing as senior associate pastor. Having been a part of Cleveland Baptist since its early days, he was loved by the people. Eventually Matt Ewing resigned from NCBC, and Dan had opportunities to fill the pulpit. Dr. Thompson had been talking with him about the possibility of becoming their pastor. In 2001, the Lord led him to Columbus, to a people with whom God had connected his heart.

Another departure was that of Greg Davis, who was both an HCS and HBI graduate. He had served as youth director and business manager. He left for Brunswick in 2004 to pastor Southwest Baptist Church. Pastor Folger's son, Peter, was brought on as youth pastor in 2001. He had been involved in bus ministry as a teen and had gone to Bible college. He had worked part-time jobs in food service and in telemarketing. He had married Sandra Elrabadi the previous year. Sandra's parents were saved in Jordan when a missionary shared the gospel with them. When they came to the United States, they settled in Lakewood and attended an Arabic-speaking Baptist church. Their pastor's son attended HCS, and it was decided that Sandra would too. She met Pete in 1992 in their sixth grade class. They were married eight years later.

One would expect Pete to have had mixed emotions when he began his full-time ministry at Cleveland Baptist. On one hand there was excitement; it was a dream come true. The church had always been his life and he was thankful for the opportunity to have a larger role in it. But having his dad as not only his pastor but also his boss could make for a complex relationship. In addition, anyone in his position might worry about the possibility of people accusing him of having his job only because of who his father was. When asked where his mind was concerning these factors, his answer was surprising: "I was too young and dumb to have put that much thought into it. I knew I loved CBC and didn't want to be anywhere else." God was certainly in it, and that made all the difference. Pete demonstrated his capability both administratively and in the pulpit and was eventually named senior associate pastor. He has overseen a number of areas of ministry, including the launch and growth of the annual Great Lakes Youth Conference.

Another hiring that would have a significant impact on the church was Ron Van Kirk's. Ron grew up in Pennsylvania. He was saved as a child, was active in ministry, and went to Pensacola Christian College to further his education. His senior year, his roommate was Tim Hanrahan. Tim had graduated from HCS in 1999, the same year as Cyndi Douglas. He told Ron about Cleveland Baptist, and Ron moved to Cleveland after graduating. He joined the church, and went to work for King's Medical Group in Hudson, Ohio.

In 2005, at age 24, Ron became the business manager of Cleveland Baptist Church. The decision to hire him required considerable foresight due to his age and the size of the church, but Ron had proven himself trustworthy and diligent in the opportunities he had been given. He had also helped with finances since Greg Davis's departure. Pastor Folger knew the Lord was leading and brought Ron up to speed on the church's financial circumstances. His first order of business was to cut spending and reduce debt (a fitting goal, as it accurately reflected his economic views as a future politician).

Even though the loan that allowed the church to build a permanent home for Heritage Christian School was miraculous, it was also costly. The same can be said for the acquisition of the Promised Land in 1999; it was both exciting and important, but also expensive. When co-pastors Roy Thompson and Kevin Folger discussed the school building project in 1991, the debt was mentioned. Dr. Thompson said, "You'll be the one inheriting all of this debt. Are you sure you want to do this?" Pastor Folger said "Yes" because he knew it was God's will.

By 2006, the financial outlook was not encouraging. Summers were the worst because there was no HCS tuition coming in, but overhead remained the same. Income was almost $50,000 behind budget by the start of school every year. The church had been paying $21,000 a month on its mortgage. If it continued at that rate, it would still be $600,000 in debt by November of 2009 when it was scheduled to be paid off. Debt would stifle the potential for growth by eliminating the possibility of expansion. Renovations would not be possible. Reaching out to the community via new streams of advertising would not be possible. Something had to be done. Pastor Folger had been senior pastor for 10 years. He had observed the explosive growth and rapid advancement of the ministry as a staff member for 25 years. He was not willing to let the church regress, so he began to pray.

Pastor Folger had become aware of an organization billing itself as a capital stewardship firm. It helped churches raise capital. He met with a representative and came away from the meeting optimistic. He scheduled a presentation after a Sunday night service in which the representative would share his plan with the deacons. In that meeting, some of the deacons asked him poignant questions. They learned that the organization wanted a substantial amount of compensation in exchange for its help in raising the money. Despite receiving a steep payment, the firm still would not cover the expenses involved in the program, such as video production, printing, and banquet meals for the church family.

Pastor Folger considered that utilizing this expensive agency might still be worthwhile if it could help the church raise a much larger sum. The meeting, however, was not productive. The deacons believed that if Pastor preached on giving and the people sought the Lord, the money could be raised without the help of an outside source. The representative had not conducted himself the way he had in his meeting with Pastor Folger, who was now discouraged because the situation was not going the way he had hoped. He asked the Lord to give the people an understanding of the need.

The option of using that particular organization had gone out the window. Pastor Folger was burdened. The financial need was significant, but he did not want to overextend his people. They were already tithing and honoring their commitments to Faith Promise Missions. Cleveland Baptist Church was filled with blue collar, hard-working people who earned modest incomes. Cleveland was not an especially affluent place.

In a day when so many Americans excuse their disinterest in serving God by saying, "All those church people want is your money," finance is a sensitive topic. The Bible says that one cannot serve both God and mammon (Matthew 6:24) and that the love of money is the root of all evil (I Timothy 6:10). Jesus stated in Matthew 6:21, "where your treasure is, there will your heart be also." People who appreciate God's sacrifice for them are willing to sacrifice for Him. What a person spends his money on reveals what he truly loves. Phrases like, "Put your money where your mouth is" exist for a reason. Finances represent livelihood.

Whether or not one believes in a cause can be measured by his willingness or unwillingness to risk his livelihood for it.

No pastor wants to constantly ask for money, but no church can expand without resources. People sometimes think they can't afford to give, but God always blesses the giver with more than that which he gave. This is why it is more blessed to give than to receive (Acts 20:35). It wasn't just the command of God that His people give, but it was also a matter of integrity. Proverbs 11:3 says, "The integrity of the upright shall guide them." When one makes a promise to pay back a loan but doesn't, his lack of integrity is demonstrated. For these reasons, Pastor Folger wanted the church's loans paid back just as the ones from the Lawson Milk Company were paid back many years earlier. The integrity of the church was at stake.

With these considerations in mind, Pastor Folger asked CBC member Chris Ruscitto to oversee an in-house capital stewardship program. Chris was a financial officer for the Cleveland Clinic, a Sunday school teacher, and a parent of four HCS students. He had professional experience in this realm that would prove to be immensely valuable.

Pastor Folger told Chris that he did not want to continue paying $21,000 a month for three years, still be $600,000 in debt, and then have to finance the remaining $600,000. They agreed that they were certainly going to have to undertake a fundraising project to obtain an additional $600,000 over a three-year period. But God gave both of them further wisdom when they asked, "Why stop there?"

Projects aimed at getting out of debt are often the least successful because there is no tangible carrot dangling. People are more likely to give toward something they can visualize;

something they can see and *have*. The ministry did have other needs, and it would not make sense to finish one campaign only to immediately begin another. They decided to combine the needs and ask for $1 million. The additional $400,000 would go to projects that would generate excitement. The bus fleet needed to be updated. This was an idea that would hook the interest of CBC's approximately 75 bus workers. Many of the church's people were burdened for missions, so the purchase and development of temporary housing for missionaries when they are off the field would be well supported. Finally, a renovated auditorium was a need that pertained to everybody. The church's bright orange look was decades old and was in desperate need of a makeover.

Pastor Folger preached on faith in both morning and evening services throughout the year. He incorporated the theme of sacrificial giving into his sermons in the months leading up to the introduction of the program. The plans were finalized in the fall of 2006, and the project was rolled out in December, just in time for the Christmas offering. Pastor Folger chose to apply the theme, "Faith: the Bridge to our Future." He cast his vision. He prayed. He hoped. However, the decision would be up to the people. Whether or not the campaign would be successful would hinge on whether or not they felt it was important enough to sacrifice. Ultimately it depended on God providing them with resources and moving in their hearts to ask them for those resources.

Commitments were taken on December 10th. The plan was for the members to give 10 percent of their capital stewardship gift via the annual Christmas offering, which would be taken on Christmas Eve. Cards indicating funds pledged were distributed, filled out, and returned. When the pledges were tallied, Cleveland Baptist Church had promised to give $1.2 million over three years. While the church was brimming with excitement, it would still have to "put its money where its mouth is."

Satan tends to attack in the aftermath of God's great victories in the lives of His children. In the subsequent years, several of Cleveland Baptist's most faithful families moved to other states. While some continued to send capital stewardship commitments, others didn't. Making matters worse was the massive economic recession that hit the United States during the campaign. Toward the end of the three-year period, the U.S. economy hit its biggest slump since the Great Depression. The bottom fell out of the real estate market as property values plummeted. Areas like Cleveland, lacking diversity in their economic portfolios, were hit especially hard. Members of the church lost their jobs. Many were financially strapped, but with God all things are possible.

There were times when progress seemed to slow, but giving remained steady. By March of 2009, the mortgage was completely paid off. It was a "Hallelujah" moment in the life of the church. Pastor Folger literally burned the document on the platform during a church service. He also leaped in the air and clicked his heels in front of the entire church as history was made. It was an unfathomable triumph considering the circumstances. God's timing was impeccable, and the blessing of having a pastor who walks with God proved critical. If the campaign hadn't been held and the remaining $600,000 had required financing, it would have been disastrous due to the economic crisis. If the church had a pastor who was not sensitive to God's leading, it would have been crippled by debt.

At the end of three years, the amount raised was not quite $1 million, but there was enough money to accomplish all of the tasks that were planned. Fortunately, some of the expenses came in under their projected cost. The price of the remodeled auditorium was less than the original estimate. In 2006, the ceiling and lighting in the auditorium had been improved, but in September of 2009, it was renovated and given a modern, crisp look. The new pews were maroon and the platform was updated with maroon, carpeted steps. The orange carpet at the top of the platform was replaced with a wooden finish. The trim was a sharp, bright white that brought vibrancy to the atmosphere. The two outside columns of pews were angled toward the center to provide maximum visibility of the preacher. Services were held in the Fellowship Hall and gymnasium during this time, including revival meetings with Evangelist Paul Schwanke.

Steve Triplett became HCS's fifth principal in 2008. He had grown up at Cleveland Baptist and planned to become an architect. God interrupted his plans, however, and called him to full-time ministry when he was a teenager. He and Pete Folger graduated from HCS in the same class and both attended Crown College. Steve married Brooke Ross, earned his master's degree, and served at churches in Knoxville, Tennessee and Columbus, Ohio until the Lord directed him back to Cleveland to oversee the school from which he had graduated.

The addition of Steve Triplett allowed Bruce Witzke to transition from principal of HCS to CBC outreach director. Perhaps the largest component of outreach at Cleveland Baptist is the bus ministry. Bruce was the right man for the job because of the knowledge and experience he had accumulated in his time as a truck driver, bus worker, and soulwinner. With funds available from capital stewardship to update the bus fleet, he was tasked with identifying buses to purchase.

The amount of money the campaign budgeted for the new bus fleet was $100,000. The buses the church had were able to get the job done, but the condition they were in was declining. Bruce had begun driving buses for the church 32 years earlier, just a week after he was saved. He had been involved in the bus ministry for most of his adult life, but he had never been asked to buy buses. He did not know where to look.

According to Matthew 6:8, "…your Father knoweth what things ye have need of, before ye ask him." God met the need when Pastor Greg Davis crossed paths with Bruce Witzke on the Cleveland Baptist property one Monday morning. He was dropping off folding chairs that he had borrowed for use at Southwest Baptist Church. Bruce offered to help him unload the chairs. The two were well acquainted since Bruce had been Greg's principal and teacher years earlier.

When they finished unloading chairs, they went out to breakfast. Bruce asked Greg what he had planned for the week. Greg said he was going to Slippery Rock, Pennsylvania to buy a mini bus that Friday. He said there was a large lot 40 miles north of Pittsburgh where hundreds of buses were sold every year. Bruce wanted to join him, but Friday was his day off. He asked about going Thursday instead. Greg said he couldn't because he wanted to have his mechanic with him to check out anything he might purchase. The input of an expert before making a major investment with hard-earned money was vital. His mechanic worked Thursday and would only be available to go on Friday. Bruce said, "How about today?" He reminded Greg that CBC's mechanic, Bill Hutcherson, could join them that day.

Greg agreed, and the three of them left for Pennsylvania just a couple hours later.

As they neared their destination, they could see it from a distance. A sprawling sea of yellow was visible from the road. When they arrived, they parted ways in their respective pursuits. There were more than 300 buses in the lot, but almost all of them were scheduled to be auctioned off less than a week later. They were not for sale. Bruce stumbled on several buses that were in excellent condition. He knew the chances that he could purchase them were slim, but he inquired anyway. He approached the manager, Mark Hernandez, who told him that the buses that caught his attention were indeed headed for the auction and were not for sale.

Bruce Witzke had always been the type of person who, in various circumstances, would say, "You never know unless you try." He asked Mark to ask his boss to double check. Mark said that he was sure; there was no need to call the owner, Earl Thoma. Bruce insisted, and he asked Mark to humor him. Impatient, Mark consented and called Earl. Bruce could hear the conversation. Without consulting any records, Earl answered that the buses were designated for the auction. Mark asked him to check again. Bruce could hear papers shuffling around on Earl's desk. He waited a moment, only to hear Earl say to himself, "Would you look at that? Those few buses there *can* be sold!" Bruce then heard Earl say to Mark, "We could part with those for about $3,500 apiece." Mark protested, "Have you seen what good shape they're in? We could get two or three times that!" Mark knew that Bruce overheard the conversation, including the price mentioned, and any leverage Mark may have had in negotiating was gone.

Not only did Bruce buy all four buses for Cleveland Baptist Church, but Earl also discovered another one that could be sold. Bruce bought that one too. A couple days later, Bruce rounded up several drivers to bring the vehicles to their new home. He had replaced a third of the fleet for $17,500, just an eighth of his budget. Three months later, Bruce and Bill Hutcherson went to New Philadelphia, Ohio, to look for more. They found nothing under $7,000 and nothing matching the quality of the buses they had purchased in Slippery Rock. Bruce called Earl again and was able to acquire two more buses for $3,500. A year later, Earl allowed Bruce to purchase other buses for $4,500 when identical buses were sold at the auction for $14,000. All things considered, the church bought 15 buses, a fueling truck, a 10-passenger van, and a plow for under $100,000.

God provided in a marvelous way. The capital stewardship campaign was a huge success. The theme, "Faith: the Bridge to our Future" was lived out in a fuller sense when some of the funds were used to create blueprints for a future master plan. This allowed the church to visualize what could be on the horizon if growth continued. In retrospect, Pastor Folger said, "It was providential to do this offering when we did. Only God knew that a great recession was looming. It was nothing short of a miracle to see our church realize our goal at that time."

A wise man cannot cast down the strength of the confidence of the mighty without sacrificing something to do so.

Dan and Denise Wolvin

Greg Davis

Pete Folger

Ron Van Kirk

Steve Triplett

Capital Stewardship Commitment Card

Burning the Mortgage

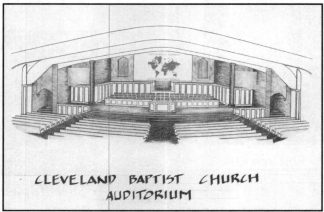

Design for Auditorium Remodel

Remodeled Auditoium

Future Expansion Plans

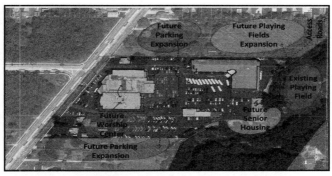

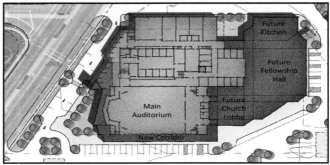

Bus Fleet

CHAPTER NINETEEN

A Temporary Farewell

We shall be like him; for we shall see him as he is.
—I John 3:2

D r. Thompson was busy after his retirement from Cleveland Baptist. He didn't stop preaching. He didn't lose his desire to get the gospel out or to help start churches. He believed that a preacher doesn't retire the way a factory or office worker does. He did not retire from the pastorate in order to spend more time on the golf course. He did not plan to put his feet up and relax. He felt that a lot of pastors question what they'll do when they retire, but he believed "there are a million things to do if you keep at it."

It didn't take long to find something to do. After his retirement in September of 1995, Dr. Thompson went to the Holy Land for three weeks. He left for the Philippines in October. His wife stayed home with the family for four months and joined him in the Philippines in January of 1996. He held revivals all over the islands and even served as an interim pastor there. He believed the Philippines were similar to the way America was in the 1950s. It was a wide open field. He and Pastor Ed Laurena had started an orphanage, and he looked forward to visiting it. He said, "Because of my upbringing, I have a real heart for children, especially children who don't have a chance." Countless Filipino children had their physical needs met and were introduced to God's plan of salvation at the orphanage.

The Thompsons returned from the Philippines in the summer of 1996. In 1997, they moved to Canada where they would live until returning to Cleveland in 2006. Their son-in-law, Al Stone, had been pastor of Bible Baptist Church in St. Thomas, Ontario, since 1989. Dr. Thompson would later spend a year serving as interim pastor at Bethel Baptist Church in Simcoe, Ontario. Over the next decade he would travel to Haiti, Ireland, the Ivory Coast, Kenya, and Russia, as well as other places. He traveled and preached extensively throughout the U.S. as well. He returned to the Cleveland Baptist pulpit numerous times for special services, including the 40th anniversary in 1998. When in Cleveland, he and his wife relished the opportunity to spend time with their children and grandchildren. They were thankful for what God was doing in their lives.

In April of 2004, a month prior to his 71st birthday, he was living in St. Thomas and had just returned from another trip to the Philippines. Despite feeling lethargic, he and his wife drove to Vermont where he would preach a revival meeting. Next they drove through a blizzard to Ajax, Ontario. He was scheduled to preach but didn't have the strength to even attend services. They went home to St. Thomas worried that he had malaria. An appointment with their family doctor was scheduled. Several hours after the appointment, the doctor called with news that they had not anticipated. Roy Thompson didn't have malaria; he had leukemia.

The doctor made arrangements for the preacher to be transported to a hospital in London, Ontario. When he got there, it was discovered that he had contracted E-Coli while overseas. With both E-Coli and leukemia, the doctors offered little hope of his survival. The family arrived within days. His granddaughters made a huge poster filled with family photos and messages of love. They had it mounted to the wall across from his bed. He later said that there were times he felt like giving up, but a look at the poster made him want to keep fighting.

God blessed Dr. Thompson with a nurse practitioner named Mark Fairweather who took a keen interest in him. The whole family forged a bond with this nurse. As encouraging phone calls came in from all over the world, Mark wondered, "Who is this guy?" Mark had been born-again, but had wandered from the Lord. Through his conversations with Roy Thompson, he re-dedicated his life to Christ. God used Roy to restore Mark's spiritual life, and He used Mark to restore Roy's physical life.

The treatment for this particular type of leukemia required three cycles of chemotherapy. One oncologist described the protocol as "walking the patient to the brink of death and then trying to walk him back." The first cycle lasted about a month. It was punishing, but it succeeded in getting the cancer into remission. Dr. Thompson was released from the hospital. Due to the effect the treatment had on his immune system, however, the number of restrictions he was given was at times overwhelming. He was highly discouraged by the thought of returning to the hospital for two more cycles of chemo. He had been through so much discomfort in the first cycle that no one could blame him for being reluctant to go back.

The second and third cycles were not as bad as the first. Roy occasionally convinced his family to smuggle him out of the hospital for an hour or two. In one instance, the hospital staff panicked and thought he was lost. They called as many of the family members as they could to inquire as to his whereabouts. He was finally found outdoors, enjoying some fresh air on the hospital campus.

When he returned home, he was still a challenging patient. The doctor's instructions were to re-admit him immediately if he developed a fever because it could be fatal. His temperature was monitored closely. One weekend, according to Faith and Joyce, "he was consuming an inordinate number of popsicles." Never having been a popsicle connoisseur in the past, something didn't seem to add up. After some investigation, it became apparent that he was trying to trick the thermometer to avoid being rushed to the hospital. His cover was blown. He was forced to spend a few more days in the hospital.

When he was in the hospital and physically able, he would grab his IV pole and go down the hall to encourage and witness to other patients. Many were staring death in the face. He knew they would listen. Some patients, nurses, and even doctors put their faith in Jesus Christ alone for salvation after talking with him. As the cancer stayed in remission, Dr. Thompson was out of the hospital again. He gradually regained strength and vitality. He started preaching again. He found that the Lord had used his medical condition to enhance his ability to empathize with others. It gave him a deeper understanding of and compassion for people in the hospital and in nursing homes. He said that if he could've battled cancer in his 30s instead of his 70s, his ministry would have benefitted from it.

Roy and his friend, Larry Clayton, took the opportunity to reminisce about praying together in the middle of the night at Akron Baptist Temple some 50 years earlier. They talked about how the Lord had given them everything they had asked of Him in those prayers. Larry's friendship was one of the greatest blessings God had given Roy Thompson.

Four years later, in 2008, the leukemia returned. At this time, he was living in Cleveland again and was treated at the Cleveland Clinic. For the second time, his cancer eventually went into remission. He was discharged in time to attend the 50th anniversary of Cleveland Baptist Church, which was celebrated on August 10th, 2008. He didn't just attend -- he preached! His message was from Genesis 1 and was titled, "God Calls His People to Remember."

Much to the dismay of everyone who knew him, his leukemia showed up again in 2009. He fought it with tenacity. He continued to read his Bible. He maintained a close walk with his Savior and an intimate prayer life. It appeared that the cancer may go into remission again. A year later he was well enough to preach, but the intensity of the battles had taken its toll. On Wednesday night, June 9th, 2010 at Grace Baptist Church in North Ridgeville, Ohio, he preached his final sermon. He was called home to heaven at 3:45 a.m. Monday morning, June 14th, less than a week later. He was 77. "Precious in the sight of the Lord is the death of His saints" (Psalm 116:15).

Dr. Thompson had touched the lives of thousands of people. Faith Thompson lost her husband of nearly 55 years. Joyce Witzke, Mark Thompson, and Ruthy Stone lost their father. Larry Clayton lost his best friend. Bob Folger lost his friend, partner, preacher, and countless other roles Roy had filled in his life. Pastor Kevin Folger lost his mentor. The older generation of Cleveland Baptist Church lost the man under whose ministry God had transformed their lives. Hearts were overwhelmed with grief, but filled with gratitude for what the Lord had done through him. His loved ones knew he was with Someone whom Philippians 1:23 calls "far better."

A favorite phrase of Roy's in the months prior to his homegoing was, "God made a bad deal." There was nothing any man could do to offset the price God paid to redeem man. As much of his life as a man may give in service to Jesus Christ, it pales in comparison to the price God paid to make salvation available to man. He was consumed by the responsibility of making as many people aware of the salvation that was offered to them as he possibly could. A statement David Gibbs remembered him saying was, "We will all walk if we can't afford gas, but we are going to reach the lost for Christ!"

Pastor Thompson's funeral was held Friday, June 18th, 2010. The remarks made left everyone in attendance in awe of what God had done through one "street kid." It was stated that he preached in more than 20 different countries and on five continents. He started churches, orphanages, schools, and medical clinics. He was a friend to mayors, governors and senators, a President, and even an emperor.

Through Christ, Roy Thompson combined humility, selflessness, and generosity with dynamic boldness. He truly loved to give. His daughters, Joyce and Ruthy, spoke as a duo. Making comments alternately, they said, "He had been befriended by statesmen and dignitaries, yet he saw just as much worth in a Haitian beggar." They spoke about how he gave freely, cared genuinely, prayed fervently, worshipped sincerely, preached boldly, lived joyfully, fought valiantly, and loved and was loved deeply.

Two of Roy's grandsons, Matt and Ben Witzke, recollected humorous memories involving their grandpa. Their testimonies showed his personal side. He was more than just a preacher -- he was fun and playful. They talked about his antics on the putt-putt course, his love for ice cream, his comically inadequate plumbing skills, his "trailblazing" driving habits, and his boyish impatience with regard to the opening of Christmas gifts.

At Dr. Thompson's request, the song, "His Life for Mine" was sung. His son Mark gave a eulogy that recounted details of Roy Thompson's life that few, if any, previously knew. It was insightful, powerful, and stirring. He read the letter that Roy's father had written in 1949 that informed the Army of Roy's age and actual identity. He told the audience that, decades earlier, his father set his own salary. He didn't want it to consume the budget or prevent the church from supporting more missionaries, so he set it very low, which forced him to trust God to provide for his family. Mark told a story about a time when the church was in hot water financially. Though the public was unaware of the problem, someone his dad had never met called him, gave him an address, and said there was something there he wanted to give to the church. He took his son, Mark, with him. In the milk chute was a paper bag containing $40,000 cash. The inside information that Mark provided made it the most memorable funeral many of Cleveland Baptist's people had ever attended.

Dr. Thompson's personality was unforgettable. As Pastor Folger put it, "He was larger than life." Gene Piazza had the opportunity to pray with him at Sunday morning men's prayer meetings. He said, "When Dr. Thompson prayed, it felt like Jesus Christ was physically right there with us." Al Stone said that he was "a preacher's preacher and the hero of the little guy."

According to Faith Thompson, "He was a lot of fun. He loved to laugh. He loved kids. He just had a heart for people. There was never a missionary that came by that he didn't take him out for ice cream. We often had people live with us. Our house was always open. He would tell me that he had invited a few people over after church and when we would arrive there would be 30 people. He wanted to give. Because of the way he grew up, never having had much, never being able to give anything, as a pastor, dad, and husband, he was a very giving person. The Lord never lets you go unrewarded for being a giver. You can't outgive Him."

Among those sorely grieving the loss of Dr. Thompson was his right-hand man, Bob Folger. On the day of the funeral, Bob was less than a week from turning 81. He had done almost every job one could do at Cleveland Baptist Church. He had been a bus driver, a bus mechanic, a bus director, a school principal, a business manager, an usher, a youth director, and a soulwinner.

Bob officially retired in 2000, but there was a running joke among the staff that he had retired three times. His life echoed the sentiments of I Corinthians 16:15, which describes those that "have addicted themselves to the ministry of the saints." Even during the times when he had no official title, job description, or salary, he could still be found on the property almost every day. Having experience and wisdom, he was a mentor to the younger men in the ministry. He gave advice to his son and grandson. Pete quipped, "He didn't think we could run things without him. He thought everything would fall apart if he didn't check on us."

By 2012, Bob's health was declining. He was still in all three church services every week. He was at men's prayer meeting every Sunday morning at 7:00 a.m. He was still preaching in the nursing homes on Monday nights. He was never a shut-in. He never lived in a nursing home. He never needed a walker. But in February it was discovered that he had lymphoma. It wasn't a long, drawn-out struggle; it happened fairly quickly. On April 5th at the age of 82, he drew his last breath.

Two days before the homegoing of his father, Pastor Folger wrote, "My dad taught me so much about living, and now he is teaching me about dying with grace and dignity." All the way to the end, Bob Folger displayed a spirit of warmth and joyfulness. He was always smiling, always friendly, and always quoting the Word.

Through the church's 54-year history to that point, he had missed very few services. He epitomized faithfulness and consistency. He genuinely loved the Lord and wanted to serve Him. He didn't need attention. He didn't need accolades. When credit was given to others instead of him, he truly was not bothered by it. Most of what he did was behind the scenes, and he liked it that way. According to his son, "He was real. There was nothing phony about him. His sincerity is what allowed him to honor God and make a difference for Him."

Bob Folger was practical. Dan Wolvin said that Dr. Thompson told him *what* to do, but Bob Folger told him *how* to do it. He and Dr. Thompson complemented each other. Pastor Thompson was the visionary. God gave him ideas. He turned his ideas over to Bob, who figured out how to put them into practice.

In addition to serving Christ through Cleveland Baptist Church, Bob was a faithful and loving husband to Nancy for

57 years. He loved his three children, grandchildren, and great grandchildren. He loved his twin brother, Dick. At Bob's funeral, Dick said, "Bob finally beat me at something. He got to heaven first." He loved his younger brother, Skip, and his sisters. Bob loved to collect and restore antique cars. He loved baseball and as a Clevelander, that meant he loved the Indians. Pete observed that though his grandfather rooted for the Indians, "During most games, he would call his brother, Dick, to complain about every managerial decision that was made."

Bob led his youngest daughter, Vicky, to the Lord when she was 10. She lost her husband 16 years later, when her two boys, Josh and Steven, were six and three. The family was living in Maryland at the time. They returned to Cleveland and Bob, affectionately known as "Gramps," profoundly influenced them. He understood the need for someone to stand in the gap and fill the void in the lives of Josh and Steven. He demonstrated proper Christian manhood to them.

Words could not express the appreciation Nancy, Brenda, Kevin, Vicky, and Cleveland Baptist Church had for the life of Bob Folger. He loved his Lord, his family, and his church deeply. In his funeral service, his son opened the Bible and read from Acts 11, where a man named Barnabas was said to have exhorted people to "cleave unto the Lord with purpose of heart." Barnabas was also said to be "a good man, and full of the Holy Ghost and of faith." Pastor Folger compared his dad to Barnabas for having exemplified the exact same characteristics.

Between 2009 and 2013, the deaths of Roy Thompson and Bob Folger weren't the only ones that affected Cleveland Baptist Church. Wally Moser, a long-time member and a close friend of Pastor Thompson's, went home to be with the Lord, as did Dr.

Harry Strachan. Dr. Strachan was the son of a missionary to the lumberjacks of northern Canada. He was a successful salesman before surrendering to full-time ministry. He had pastored three different churches, including the one in which Al Stone grew up, the same one for which Dr. Thompson served as interim pastor.

In 1995, Dr. Strachan was asked to oversee Heritage Baptist Institute. In his dignified and God-honoring manner, he trained young men and women in the finer points of ministry. He took his job seriously. He taught classes, gave counsel, organized chapel services, and preached the Word of God. As his health began to deteriorate, Luke Brown assumed an increasing number of responsibilities regarding HBI. On January 4th, 2010, at the age of 81, Dr. Strachan graduated to heaven.

As Cleveland Baptist pushed beyond 50 years in ministry, God was calling its first generation of servants off the scene. Every time another person who had been around for most of the life of the church passed away, the younger generation lost a link to its beginnings. The younger members hadn't gone through the struggles of growing the membership by the hundreds that the older generation had. Those who remained had a responsibility to move forward, but to do so while remembering the sacrifices made by those who came before them. This would not be an easy task because the ones who work for something are usually the ones who appreciate its value. While the crowd that remained had its own unique battles to fight, it hadn't gone through the process of outgrowing a house, a theater building, buying property, or the legalities of opening a school. Remembering the hard-fought victories of its past would be the key to Cleveland Baptist's future.

When wise men scale a city, their imprint is left on lives when their work is over.

The Members of the Cleveland Baptist Church
gratefully remember their Pastor,
Friend and Servant of 37 years

REV. HENRY ROY THOMPSON, D.D.

His life was a shining example of dedication to the Gospel of Jesus Christ.

His legacy is the countless number of people in America and around
the world who have benefitted from his caring and ceaseless efforts,
who will in turn carry on with the unfinished work.

Romans 8:38-39

Cleveland Baptist Church, 4431 Tiedeman Road, Brooklyn, OH 44144
216-671-2822   www.clevelandbaptist.org

One More Thing About Henry Roy Thompson...

My family appreciated the Obituary article on my father, Henry Roy Thompson, in the June 18 Plain Dealer, and all the tributes that have come in to the PD, to other online forums, and directly to the family. Many wonderful things have been written and spoken. The family also wishes to pay tribute, and we wish to do so by remembering something important about Dad that has often been underemphasized or overlooked- though Dad was considered a "conservative" fellow, his life was one of true diversity. Perhaps there is a lesson here – perhaps we are too anxious to label everyone as either right or left, liberal or conservative, exclusive or inclusive. Maybe it isn't that simple.

There was never a need for a federal judge to order my father to racially integrate his church. He just did it. Visitors during Dad's calling hours and funeral were White, Black, East Asian, South Asian, Native American, Hispanic, Gypsy, Middle Eastern and other. All treating each other with respect and love, just as my father had shown toward them.

Congress did not need to pass a bill telling Cleveland Baptist Church that it should provide free transportation and access to the economically disadvantaged or physically challenged. The Church just did it. There was nothing more uplifting to our family last week than to witness the extraordinary effort of so many wheelchairbound folks to

come and pay their respects to Dad. Our hearts were touched as we listened carefully to dozens of deaf people doing the best they could to verbally communicate their love for my father and their appreciation of his concern for them.

No pundit needed to pressure Dad and his congregation to provide multi-lingual services or offer free use of facilities to those to whom English was a foreign language. It was simply done without fanfare.

It was not necessary for a social agency to beg Dad to take in a Jewish family during the mass migration from the Soviet Union. He just went and offered, and then hosted a family in his home for more than a year. When they left, he gave them my mother's car.

Dad gave to the homeless his whole life, not for photo-ops or in response to

fundraising efforts, but quietly and privately in response to phone pleas from men and women he didn't know, but whom he knew were desperate for help.

There was no waiting for the State Department to figure out the best way to distribute taxpayer-funded aid to foreign countries. For 37 years, Dad sacrificed extras at home so that he and the Church could always send money and personnel to poor nations, then in "retirement" sent himself and his faithful wife to start orphanages and schools among the poorest of the poor.

So hopefully it is obvious that even though Dad was proud to be called a "conservative," the deeds of his lifetime are irrefutable evidence that the term meant something different to him than it does to many others, particularly in the polarized media of our day. He was a forceful man, sometimes prone to overstatement, but that should not distort his record of compassion which far surpasses that of all but a very few. His life illuminates a truth Dad always believed and taught both in word and by example: that whatever the proper role of collective benevolence, true charity and liberality are matters of individual conscience and duties of individual action, and the more of us that practice the same, the better off our country will be.

Mark D. Thompson

"Doc" Harry Strachan

Bob Folger

CHAPTER TWENTY

A Momentous Task

…his spirit was stirred in him, when he saw the city wholly given to idolatry. —Acts 17:16

Romans 1:16 says that the gospel of Christ "is the power of God unto salvation." Salvation means being saved from sin and its condemnation in hell. The verse goes on to say that this salvation is available "to everyone that believeth." The gospel itself is simply the death, burial, and resurrection of Jesus Christ as the "just for the unjust." Jesus was without sin, yet He was punished as though He was the worst of sinners. The sin of mankind was placed upon Him and He bore the punishment for it all. He "tasted death for every man" (Hebrews 2:9).

Philippians 3:9 adds that a person can "be found in him," not having his "own righteousness." To be saved, Romans 3:26 states that one must receive Jesus Christ's righteousness. His sinless righteousness is offered as a free gift that cannot be earned (Romans 5:18). One may receive this free gift by choosing to "acknowledge the truth" (II Timothy 2:25) that God became man, lived without sin, died, and rose again, according to the Scriptures. Those who choose to accept this gift have their sins forgiven (Acts 10:43) and become a child of God (John 1:12). They were born the first time *physically*, but when they receive eternal life by believing on Christ (John 5:24), they are born again *spiritually* (John 3:3, 7). This is referred to in the New Testament repeatedly as being "saved."

Jesus Christ, as the Head of every proper church, has given each believer the responsibility of reaching its city with the above message. The church is never told to *force* anyone to believe. That is impossible. When Jesus preached, some believed and some didn't. When the apostles preached, some believed and some didn't. To be saved, one must be "fully persuaded in *his own* mind" (Romans 14:5) because he will "give account of *himself* to God" (Romans 14:12). It is the work of the Holy Spirit to convict individuals of their sin and their corresponding need of salvation (John 16:8). The Holy Spirit draws all men to Christ (John 12:32). Because "the grace of God that bringeth salvation hath appeared to all men," (Titus 2:11) each individual is responsible for his choice as to whether he receives or refuses the gospel and the salvation it brings.

The task of presenting the truth to every person in a city and confronting each individual with the choice before him is a momentous one. God never said it would be easy. In fact, the men who first took this message to the world were told to forsake all of the comforts and conveniences they had and "hazard their lives" (Acts 15:26) for "my sake, and the gospel's" (Mark 8:35). All they were promised was that men would "revile you, and persecute you," and "say all manner of evil against you falsely, for my sake" (Matthew 5:11).

When Dr. Thompson started Cleveland Baptist Church, he didn't expect it to be easy, and it wasn't. Joy, peace, and contentment come from obeying God. Dr. Thompson obeyed God by doing what God told him to do. As a wise man scaling the city of the mighty and casting down the strength of the confidence thereof, thousands of men were reached. There are still others clinging to their own strength and might. The church must reach them. They are asking, "How can I, except some man should guide me?" (Acts 8:31) Romans 10:14 asks, "How shall they hear without a preacher?"

Despite living in a day that fulfills God's promise of perilous times coming (II Timothy 3:1), Cleveland Baptist remains committed to the same goals it has had since 1958. Every day, its mission is to exalt Christ by honoring His command to make His salvation known to the lost souls in Cleveland, Ohio. The example Paul set for the church in its attitude toward people was to "very gladly spend and be spent" for them (II Corinthians 12:15). The prayer of Cleveland Baptist Church is that no person in the city would say, "No man cared for my soul" (Psalm 142:4).

In 2012 and 2013, more was accomplished for the purpose of yielding to Christ as He seeks and saves "that which was lost" (Luke 19:10) in a city of the mighty. Reaching more people requires more space to operate. The church had been trying to purchase the property to its north for years. The owner, however, insisted on asking $375,000 for it. Paying more for it than it was worth would not have been wise stewardship, so the church was patient.

When the owner passed away, his family took over the estate. The church had the property appraised, and its value was shown to be far less than previously discussed. With the house empty and the family anxious to sell, Cleveland Baptist Church was able to purchase the property in March of 2012 for $168,000. This acquisition, made possible through the sacrificial giving of the people, will accommodate expansion designed to facilitate a ministry that reaches an increased number of lost souls.

Recognizing that Cleveland is not comprised of solely English-speaking people and that all people need Christ regardless of linguistic differences, another change was made in 2012. Jose Duarté was brought in from Utah to re-launch the church's Spanish ministry, which was started in 1991. Its origins can be traced back to the salvation of Dave Miranda, who heard the gospel for the first time at a kindergarten graduation at a Baptist church in Brunswick, Ohio in 1984. Looking for a church closer to his home, he was directed to Cleveland Baptist. Through the preaching of God's Word, he allowed the Lord to conform him to His image. He became a fervent soulwinner and developed a sincere burden for the lost.

Dave could speak Spanish, and by 1991, the Lord was prompting his heart to add a Spanish outreach to Cleveland Baptist Church. The majority of the city's Spanish-speaking population was either Catholic or Pentecostal. Due to the error found in these belief systems, most of the Spanish-speaking people of Cleveland believed that receiving and keeping salvation was based on their works. Dave enlisted the help of Brian Starre, the church's outreach director at the time. Dave interpreted while Brian preached. Sometimes Pastor Thompson or other preachers would address the group.

In 2001, God called Brian Starre and his wife to a ministry which helps churches grow in their knowledge of the Scriptures by providing study curriculum and discipling believers.

Leadership in the Spanish ministry was given to Don Weeks. Don eventually left to take the gospel to Bolivia. Upon his departure, Jim Jones took over. Jim had recently been on a missions trip to Cuba that touched his heart for Spanish-speaking people. While Jim loved the people and served them wholeheartedly, he was not bilingual. The department shrank.

By 2009, those who still attended were able to clearly understand the sermons in English. It didn't make sense to keep them separate from the auditorium when they did not require translation. Sadly, the ministry disbanded. Pastor Folger and the church prayed for God to send them a man who didn't require an interpreter and had strong convictions on the fundamentals of the faith and separation from the world. The Lord answered this prayer by bringing Pastor Jose Duarté to Cleveland in January of 2012. He, his wife, and their children immediately began knocking on doors in the areas of the city with high concentrations of Spanish speakers. Attendance steadily climbed, and the Lord has made it a highly fruitful ministry.

In addition to those who do not understand English, Cleveland Baptist cares about those who cannot hear. Its deaf ministry is one of the features of the church that makes it stand out to first-time visitors. A sign language interpreter in a mini pulpit on the side of the platform allows hearing-impaired individuals to understand each sermon. In over 45 years of ministry, hundreds of deaf people have received Christ as their Savior.

The deaf ministry is led by Pastor Bob Mickey. Bob is not deaf, but has been challenged in the realm of hearing since his childhood in Pennsylvania. After he was married, he and his wife, Janet, moved to Cleveland. Neither of them was saved. They were led to Christ at a Southern Baptist church before becoming members at Cleveland Baptist. Bob got connected with the deaf ministry by driving a bus to pick them up for church. He has led this group for more than 35 years.

It isn't enough to reach only English-speaking people in Cleveland. Nor is it enough to reach the city's Spanish, deaf, and Gypsy speakers (which it started doing in the late 1980s). To obey the command of Christ, Cleveland Baptist Church is responsible for reaching the entire world, which includes speakers of thousands of other languages.

Throughout its history, Cleveland Baptist has had a part in worldwide missions through a program called Faith Promise Missions. A concept that swept through churches affiliated with the BBF in the '60s, the program calls for a church's people to promise a certain dollar amount beyond their tithe each year. The promise is made at an annual missions conference in which missionaries are present to give testimonies and presentations, preach, and encourage believers to be involved through prayer. Each member is expected to earnestly seek the Lord to ask Him for a specific amount of money to pledge. When the promise is made, the believer, through faith, acknowledges that he will give that amount regardless of any changes that are made that year in his personal financial picture. The funds are pooled and issued in a fixed amount per month to various missionaries. It is a way to organize giving that demands faith and simultaneously reaches souls around the globe.

Cleveland Baptist's missions giving year begins in May and runs through the following April. From May 2012 to April 2013, the church gave over $500,000 to worldwide missions for the first time in its history. This was especially impressive considering it was in the midst of paying off the recently purchased property to the north. This was made possible when the Holy Spirit prompted Pastor Folger to take $1,000 out of the general fund each week and give it to missions.

One might wonder how $1,000 a week can make a substantial difference. The answer is simple: the higher the amount in the missions budget, the more missionaries the church can support. With an additional $52,000 a year in the budget, the church can have a part in the ministry of far more missionaries than it could without it. A church that doesn't give as much to missions may be able to support just a handful of missionaries, whereas Cleveland Baptist supports well over 100 missionaries.

While a man who scales a city to cast down the strength of its confidence is wise, there are other cities that must be scaled. Other wise men must be sent. Physically, a man can be only in one city at one time. Through giving and prayer, he can support wise men that God sends to other cities.

In Ecclesiastes 9:14-16, Solomon speaks again of a wise man's role in a city. Written later in his life than Proverbs 21:22 was written, he has something to add to it. It is possible that he is referring to the actual events of a city called Abel of Beth-maachah mentioned in II Samuel 20:14-22. Of Ecclesiastes 9:14-16, a comparison to Christ's ministry could also be made. Regardless of whether he is giving a parable, a real history, or a Messianic prophecy, he adds another layer to the verse on which the theme of this book is based. In this instance, he is not talking about the necessity of wisdom being employed to seize a city. Rather, the passage considers defense as opposed to offense:

> *There was a little city, and few men within*
> *it; and there came a great king against it, and*

*besieged it, and built great bulwarks against it: Now
there was found in it a poor wise man, and he by his
wisdom delivered the city; yet no man remembered
that same poor man. Then said I, Wisdom is better
than strength: nevertheless the poor man's wisdom
is despised, and his words are not heard.*

Solomon realized that wisdom is seldom remembered,
even when it was wisdom that delivered a city. There is no doubt
that it is the Lord Jesus Christ who builds His church and delivers
His people. There is, however, a sense in which the people of
Cleveland Baptist Church were delivered from worldliness and
sin through the ministry of wise men. In this case, the wise men
were those described in the previous pages. They were wise
because they lifted up, taught, applied, and obeyed God's Word.

The precious Word of God is the only source of pure wisdom.
Through Solomon, God reminds His people that those who
offer difference-making wisdom are easy to forget. This is not
because they are not memorable. It is because sinful man has
a tendency toward ingratitude; he forgets why he has what he
has. Simply because it is easy to forget them does not mean that
God's people *should* forget them. To the contrary, they should
remember them.

This book was written to the end that the wisdom of godly
men in Cleveland not be forgotten.

Bob Mickey and the Deaf Ministry

Duarte Family

Present Day

Pastor and Denise Folger

Folger Family